Making Life HAPPEN!

A Compilation of Heartwarming
and Passionate Lessons Learned
From the Life of Marlene Evans

© 2007
CHRISTIAN WOMANHOOD
8400 Burr Street
Crown Point, Indiana 46307
www.christianwomanhood.org
(219) 365-3202

ISBN: 0-9793892-7-5

CREDITS:
Section 1 and 3 Photographs:
Courtesy of Larry Titak Photography

Section 2 Photograph:
Gatlinburg, Tennessee
Standing: Jean Henderson, Marlene Evans, Renee Cox
Seated: Nan Davis

Section 4 Photograph:
Courtesy of Ruth Allen

Layout and Design: Linda Stubblefield
Proofreaders: Rena Fish, Jane Grafton, Cindy Schaap

All Scripture references used in this book
are from the King James Bible.

Printed and Bound in the United States

Dedication

This book is lovingly dedicated to Doris Smith, Marlene Evans' sister, and to Dianne Dowdey, Doris Smith's daughter and Marlene Evans' niece.

Jerry & Doris Smith

I admire Doris Smith for many reasons. Though she is a completely different personality than her older sister, in her own way she has been as much of a role model to me as Marlene Evans. I also admire the way Doris supported her sister who was in the limelight. There was never jealousy for the attention her sister received; there was never impatience with the many people who came to their pew in church to get a hug, an autograph, or an encouraging word from her sister; and there was never anger or bitterness toward these people because their presence took away from the precious limited time she was able to spend with her sister. Doris quietly supported her well-known sister with love and kindness.

Dianne Dowdey was very close to her "Aunt Marlene." They laughed together, talked together, and seemed like true "soul mates." More Sundays than not, I receive a note under my office door at the

Chip, Dianne, Chad, and Ben Dowdey

church from Dianne. I believe those notes come partially because I have assumed responsibility for Christian Womanhood, the ministry that Marlene Evans started in 1976. I love Dianne and appreciate her thoughtfulness and kindness to me. No one could ever "replace" Marlene Evans in Christian Womanhood, but Dianne has made me feel very secure that she is pleased with the direction Christian Womanhood is going.

Doris and Dianne both have shown tremendous support of all the people who have worked to perpetuate the work that Marlene Evans began. I want to thank them for their support and their loyalty; these are two godly women whom I admire and love very much!

– Cindy Schaap
Senior Editor
Christian Womanhood

Acknowledgments

As the senior editor of *Christian Womanhood*, I wanted this book to be written. The teachings of Marlene Evans are too life-changing to simply be left in the archives of cassette tapes and *Christian Womanhood* issues of the past. The only way to prevent this from happening is for those of us who know her and knew her well to keep her memory alive. I am excited about this book because it is chock-full of simple, yet profound truths to help us live life to the fullest—especially in the area of relationships.

I want to thank those who helped to make this book a reality. First, my heartfelt thanks to each person who wrote a chapter. You remembered stories about Marlene Evans that delightfully share her unique personality, and in the telling of that fraction of her life, we can all learn.

I want to thank Jane Grafton for finding time in a busy schedule to write lessons to learn at the end of each chapter. Many times it is difficult for some people to read a story and readily grasp a truth from the printed page. Jane has made it easier for us to apply the truth of each story to our own lives. I am very grateful for her labor of love in helping to keep the vibrant life of Marlene Evans alive.

Thank you to Linda Stubblefield for collecting the stories and dividing them into appropriate units for the book. My thanks to Rena Fish for proofreading this tribute to Marlene Evans.

Thank you, dear reader, for joining me in remembering the passionate life of a lady I greatly loved and admired.

– Cindy Schaap

BOOKS BY MARLENE EVANS

A Daily Chat Around the Bible With Marlene Evans
Cancer: My Enemy, My Friend
Christian Womanhood Cookbook
Comfort for Hurting Hearts
Help Lord! They Call Me Mom
I'm Going to Live Until I Die (booklet)
Memories of Malaumanda (booklet)
Redbirds and Rubies and Rainbows
The Five Sins of Christian Women
There's Life After Cancer

THE LIFE SERIES
Kids Without Chaos
Marriage Without Divorce
Relationships Without Regrets
Sickness Without Despair
Teens Without Turmoil

COMPILATIONS BY MARLENE EVANS
New Hope: Be the Parent You Were Meant to Be
Pattern for Living
Pattern for Living Teacher's Manual

Mrs. Evans' life story is chronicled in the book
Marlene Evans: A Biography
by Jane Grafton

Table of Contents

Introduction by Cindy Schaap 11
Who Was Marlene Evans? by Carol Tudor 13
Foreword by Jane Grafton 21

Section 1—Mind Control / 25

Just Another Sunday by Ruby Velez 27
Mrs. Evans Said…and I Knew What to Do
    by Zana Reichen 33
Life Ain't Fair by Leslie Beaman .37
Crippled With Fear by Leslie Beaman 41
How to Get Over Your Hurts Fast by Loretta Walker 43
My Circle of Protection by Leslie Beaman 47
A Visit From the Preacher by Linda Stubblefield 49
Chasing the Redbirds by Leslie Beaman 53
Life's Changes by Leslie Beaman .55
Thanks for Listening by Zana Reichen 57
My View From the Ditch by Leslie Beaman 59
Her Silence Spoke Volumes—During Critical Times
    by Leslie Beaman 63
A Southern Belle Wannabe by Leslie Beaman 67

Section 2—Building Happy Relationships / 71

Woman the Adjuster by Loretta Walker 73
"I Speak Simpson" by Leslie Beaman 77
Be Everyone's Cheerleader by Zana Reichen 81
Building Strong Relationships by Kris Grafton 85

The Importance of People by Jane Grafton 89
I Can't Understand by Rena Fish 91
The Importance of Being Friendly by Gina Eyer 95
Are You Making a Difference? by Gina Eyer 97
She Tuned in to Others by Dianne Dowdey 101
She Registered Approval by Dianne Dowdey 105
Waiting in the Wings by Leslie Beaman 107
Don't Take Up My Cause by Leslie Beaman 111
Anger by Leslie Beaman 115
Life's Distractions by Leslie Beaman 117
A Round Table Discussion by Leslie Beaman 121
Her Silence Spoke Volumes—When Correcting
    by Leslie Beaman 125
Did I Tell You I Am Going to Die Soon?
    by Leslie Beaman 127
Being Gracious by Julie Busby 129

Section 3—Principles for Life / 131

Finding the Best in Others by Doris Smith 133
Practicing How to Talk by Carol Tudor 135
Lessons on Speaking From Marlene Evans
    by Frieda Cowling 137
Mrs. Evans—The Life Changer by Leslie Beaman 139
Who's Crowing in Your Life? by Leslie Beaman 143
Red Car Fever by Leslie Beaman 145
We Just Don't Complain! by Linda Stubblefield 147
Making a Mark by Leslie Beaman 151
Marlene Evans, My Boss by Linda Meister 153
Rubies—A Reminder by Frieda Cowling 157
After All These Years, I Can Still Hear Her Voice!
    by Leslie Beaman 161
Speed Bumps by Leslie Beaman 163

Veto Power by Leslie Beaman 165
Stay Away From Fish Sticks and Green Jello
    by Leslie Beaman 169
Are You Sick or What? by Leslie Beaman 173
I Want You to Be at Peace by Leslie Beaman 177

Section 4—Making Life Happen / 181

She Hugged Life Into Me by Sheri Edwards 183
He Fills Our Mouth With Laughter by Leslie Beaman . . .185
Be a Different Woman! by Frieda Cowling 189
God Colors My Hair by Frieda Cowling 193
Never Underestimate the Value of One Black Skirt
    by Kristal Slager 195
A Catastrophic Road Trip by Kristal Slager 199
My Memory of Marlene Evans by Tina Lashbrook 207
Time-Released Teaching by Frieda Cowling 209
Marlene Evans—The Atmosphere Setter
    by Frieda Cowling 211
Marlene Evans Moments by Nancy Musser 215
Honk...if You Love Coffee! by Leslie Beaman 217
The Candy Jar Is Empty by Leslie Beaman 221

Afterword

by Joan Lindish 223

Introduction
by Cindy Schaap

Marlene Evans had a very multi-textured personality which God used to influence thousands of women in many different ways in their Christian lives. She was a very fun person with a delightful personality, but she was also a woman who had memorized much Scripture and studied the Bible with diligence and intellect. She was a person who loved to talk; yet, she was one of the best listeners I have ever known. Her body was stricken with cancer, and while she faced her enemy and did what she could to be in the best health possible, she did not talk her poor health; she focused on what she **could** do. Because of these attributes, I wanted Christian Womanhood to publish a book that would be both entertaining and educational to capture her personality.

Marlene Evans made life happen on purpose because of the discipline and lessons she had learned in her own life. I hope not only that this book captures her personality and knowledge, but that it also captures the lessons that helped her make life happen through 19 years of fighting cancer.

Who Was Marlene Evans?

by Carol Tudor

Marlene Evans believed a woman's top priority was completing the men God placed in her life. If she were here right now I believe she'd say she learned that from Dr. Jack Hyles, the pastor of First Baptist Church of Hammond, Indiana, for 41 years. Mrs. Evans said more than once, "I am in a position of influence because of my husband." She often referred to her husband, Dr. Wendell Evans; her dad, Alvin Zugmier; her college president, Dr. Bob Jones, Sr.; and the two main pastors of her adult life, Dr. Lee Roberson and Dr. Jack Hyles, as the men who influenced her life the most. She quoted them all DAILY!

Our pastor, Dr. Jack Schaap, said at Mrs. Evans' memorial service that she and Dr. Evans had a very unique and rare relationship. They each had individual ministries that slightly overlapped, and yet, there was never any professional jealousy or competition in their marriage. Dr. and Mrs. Evans talked at length about their schedules and speaking engagements, as Mrs. Evans wanted to be certain that she was doing what her husband wanted her to do.

Mrs. Evans also was very committed to her local church. The ladies' meetings where she spoke were usually on Friday and Saturday. She was known to fly home through the night, if need be, in order to get back in time for church on Sunday morning.

As different as she was, Mrs. Evans was as real and down-to-earth as the girl next door. She never became impressed with herself. In fact, that was one thing she hated—pretense. She loved all people, but she did admit that she had a difficult time with pretentious and "uppity" acting folks. I believe that one of the reasons God was able to trust Mrs. Evans with the responsibility of helping ladies was that she so loved and respected the individual and totally accepted each person—strengths, weaknesses, and all. There was no caste system with her. She saw all people as being equal. She resented someone's praising her for being good to a person who was slow intellectually, homeless, or whatever. She was not a respecter of persons and didn't think those types of people should be treated any differently than someone with great amounts of money or education. In fact, she went to great lengths to compensate for those of us who didn't treat these types of people the way Jesus would. She seemed to live Hebrews 13:2 which says, *"Be not forgetful to entertain strangers: for thereby some have entertained angels unawares."*

I recall one day I said, "That person is a bit strange."

She immediately responded calmly, "I wouldn't have noticed if you hadn't mentioned it."

Another time I said impatiently, "When is Susie going to get what I've been trying to teach her for all these years!?!?!"

"When we learn to eat right is when she will learn what you want her to learn," she answered.

I was stunned into silence. I realized that it sometimes takes a lifetime to develop certain habits and that I had plenty of my own areas that needed work. She helped me realize I just needed to be patient with co-workers.

Dr. and Mrs. Evans were "early-morning people," and their favorite time to be together was breakfast. They would go out early so they could have a long (sometimes even a two-hour) breakfast and talk time. They thoroughly enjoyed each other's company. What had attracted them to each other when they were dating was their ability to communicate and talk on many subjects for hours at a time. They kept that quality in their 46-plus year marriage. About two years before Mrs. Evans went to Heaven, a waitress approached them when they were eating out and said,

"Are you two married to each other?"

When they laughed and answered "Yes!" she responded, "We never see married couples laugh and talk together the way you do."

Before health problems struck both of them, they were often co-emcees of family parties. No two people could do it better! Dr. and Mrs. Evans would spend hours planning how to make their family Christmas special. Dr. Evans would lead songs around the family piano with brother-in-law, Jerry Smith, at the keyboard. They always had a game plan and would look to each other during the party for the next "happening." Dr. Evans' humor helped set a fun spirit. Mrs. Evans was the first to laugh and the one to laugh the longest, even at what some would call corny attempts at

Left to right: Doris holding Chad, Marlene and Wendell Evans, Jerry Smith at the organ

humor. I never knew her to ever put down Dr. Evans' humor. More than once in Hyles-Anderson College chapel, she would continue to laugh after others had stopped laughing at one of his jokes. He would grin and publicly say, "Thank you, Marlene!"

When I think of Dr. and Mrs. Evans' marriage, I think of these words: love, respect, unfailingly kind, acceptance of each other's idiosyncrasies, best friends, sweethearts, love of books, loyalty, and oneness.

Mrs. Evans told me when I got married, "Let Richard do whatever he wants in his own home." She lived by this philosophy. I recall one New Year's Day where she borrowed two televisions so that Dr. Evans could watch three football games at the same time. He simply turned off the volume and watched! Because he preferred not to be interrupted during these games, she had the refrigerator and kitchen well stocked with his favorite foods—including mincemeat pie—and left him to his own "devices"! This is just one example of hundreds, as she found a way to make her husband king.

Those of us who worked closely with Mrs. Evans knew that when we were on the phone with her, we could at any time hear the words, "My husband just walked in!" and "click." She tried never to be on the phone when her husband was present.

After she was diagnosed with ovarian cancer in 1994 and knew that her condition would require the help of caregivers, she worked out a way for those ladies to have a separate entrance into the house and an area away from Dr. Evans in order to protect his privacy. She found other ways to protect him, such as keeping the house quiet when he was home and asking the caregivers not to park in the driveway, so he could get in and out of the garage easily.

Both Dr. and Mrs. Evans knew they had idiosyncrasies that others would find "different." Dr. Evans would say, "But Marlene and I are a cut above other people; we *know* we're weird!" after which they would both laugh heartily.

As I mentioned already, Marlene Evans was not a respecter of persons. However, family was special. Among the instructions and thoughts Mrs. Evans left regarding her death, she had written something that pretty well stated her philosophy on family. "Relatives are relatives." Family get-togethers were exclusively for the family.

Mrs. Evans experienced an "image crisis" after the first Christian Womanhood Spectacular, an annual international ladies' conference conducted at First Baptist Church of Hammond, Indiana. She insisted on having a big party for her roots—her entire family—Sunday afternoon, the day following the Spectacular. Special food, special gifts, and special words were presented to each family member. She wanted them to know that no matter what fleeting fame she might have, her family was still number one. She continued this tradition through her last Spectacular in 2000.

Success that brought many opportunities seemed to make Mrs. Evans desire family times even more. Her niece, Dianne Dowdey, may have expressed it best when she said, "Because of the way she treated family and spent time with family, it was difficult to remember that Aunt Marlene was famous."

It is impossible to capture on page the real Marlene Evans. She was as complex as she was simple. There are so many other aspects of Mrs. Evans' life and qualities that the public did not see. Though she was a "people person," she enjoyed hours of quiet time alone at home. She was a talker, but she was also a deep thinker who meditated often and thought of unique and creative ways to transfer truth. She was a mannerly person who always said, "Please," "Thank you," "Pardon me," etc. She was careful of using these words even in the last days of her life. She was also a very modest, feminine lady.

She constantly looked for ways to be good to others, especially if she felt they had gone out to their way to help her. Just days before she passed away, I was called to her bedside late one evening to give her some medical attention. My husband drove me there, and before I left, Mrs. Evans handed me a gift certificate to Teibel's Restaurant.

Mrs. Evans had a strong desire to please, follow, and honor the preacher and his wife. When Dr. Jack Schaap became the pastor of First Baptist Church, Mrs. Evans wrote his wife a note and said, "I will be referring to you as 'Mrs. Schaap' from now on instead of 'Cindy.' It's not because of any lack of warmth on my part, but rather the fact that you are now my pastor's wife and deserve that respect." Just a few weeks before her Homegoing, she heard

Brother Schaap say in a Sunday night sermon, regarding slits in ladies' dresses, "Why don't you just sew them all up?" The next day she had one of her caregivers take all the dresses out of her closet and sent them to a seamstress to have the slits sewn up. She was always on the side of leadership.

Dr. & Mrs. Jack Schaap

She was also a very confidential person. While most people thought of her as a talker, she never betrayed the confidences of those whom she counseled.

She was a very *common*, down-to-earth woman in the way she related to women and their problems, but she lived a very *uncommon* Christian life. She talked about common problems in an uncommonly funny way. She challenged every lady to be uncommon, a princess, a queen, a different woman in her own home. She was a different woman, a larger-than-life personality who set a *new* standard for Christian ladies in America.

Carol Frye Tudor was Marlene Evans' faithful friend and colleague for 28 years. In September 1973, Carol was a 23-year-old registered nurse, studying to be a doctor. She heard Dr. Wendell Evans speak at her home church in Glenview, Illinois. Because of the sermon she heard, she visited Hyles-Anderson College and attended Mrs. Evans' Christian Womanhood class. God gave Mrs. Evans and Carol an immediate rapport with each other. Carol resigned from her nursing position and enrolled at Hyles-Anderson College.

Marlene Evans & Carol Frye Tudor

Carol worked with Mrs. Evans in the Dean of Women's Office from 1973 through 1992. Carol also worked with Mrs. Evans in the founding of Christian Womanhood in 1975. She frequently traveled and spoke with Mrs. Evans at Christian Womanhood Mini-Spectaculars until Mrs. Evans no longer traveled.

She continued nursing Mrs. Evans until her death in 2001.

Foreword
by Jane Grafton

*G*od knew He needed a woman yielded to the Holy Spirit, a woman whose wisdom would portray the mind of Christ, a woman full of good works, and a woman whose influence would touch a generation of Christian ladies. With all of this in mind, God fashioned Mrs. Marlene Evans with a unique personality, and she, in turn, humbly accepted the responsibility. As Mrs. Evans had the ear of fundamental women of America, she lovingly, wisely, and compassionately ministered to them in an attempt to help them salvage and build their homes for Christ. She graciously accepted the charge God gave her, the care of the homes of this generation, and what a difference she made!

It seems that God gives to each generation a man—a prophet—upon whom He has given "*...the care of all the churches.*" (II Corinthians 11:28) These are men such as Charles Haddon Spurgeon, Dr. John R. Rice, and Dr. Jack Hyles.

I have wondered, because we live in an era unique unto itself, could it be that God knew this generation also needed a woman—a prophetess, if you will—upon whom He could give "the care of all the homes"? If He did, God chose this woman knowing...

- the skeptic would need someone who was real
- the intellectual would need someone who was learned
- the down and out would need someone who was compassionate
- the hurting would need someone whose spontaneous fun helped her laugh through the tears
- the unsaved would need someone who was a soul winner
- the lonely would need someone who was loving

- the poor would need someone who was giving and generous
- the afflicted would need someone whose mother had polio
- the brusque would need someone who understood "Zugmier-ese" (Mrs. Evans' maiden name)
- the beautiful would need someone who kept herself and dressed attractively
- the loose and sensual would need someone who was modest and appropriate
- the rebellious would need someone who lived by her convictions
- the defeated would need someone who picked herself up after a fall
- the negative would need someone who rejoiced in the Lord
- the critical gossip would need someone who found the good in everyone
- the shy would need someone who was sensitive
- the societal reject would need someone who was accepting
- the strong would need someone who, though strong herself, submitted to leadership
- the student would need someone who was teachable
- the self-righteous would need someone who was truly spiritual
- the proud would need someone who, though famous, remained humble.

I hope as you read the attributes I wrote about Mrs. Evans, you were challenged as I was to follow her example. It's easy to think, "Well, I'm no Marlene Evans!" You're right; I'm not either. But God has given each of us people who cross our paths, live in our homes, work in our places of business, and attend our churches who need us. God has a job for each of us. Let's do it as diligently and as purposefully as Marlene Evans did hers!

You don't have to be just like Marlene Evans to be used of God and influence lives for eternity.

1. Do you know what abilities God has given you to influence others?

2. It is not prideful to evaluate the strengths God has given you. It is wise. Develop those strengths to make a difference in the lives of others.

3. Do not try to be just like someone else. Be who God planned for you to be. Oftentimes ladies get discouraged because they look at others and feel inferior in their abilities. Refuse to compare yourself to someone else. II Corinthians 10:12 states, *"For we dare not make ourselves of the number, or compare ourselves with some that commend themselves: but they measuring themselves by themselves, and comparing themselves among themselves, are not wise."*

4. Ephesians 4:11 and 12 help us see that God needs all different types of people to do His work—*"And he gave some, apostles; and some, prophets; and some, evangelists; and some, pastors and teachers; For the perfecting of the saints, for the work of the ministry, for the edifying of the body of Christ."* Learn your God-given abilities and use them to do His work!

Jane Grafton attended a mother-daughter banquet at Rosemount, Minnesota, and heard Marlene Evans speak on "The Five Sins of Christian Women." She left the meeting that night with a passion to become a "different woman" like Mrs. Evans had described—a woman who was kind to everyone, who dressed modestly, who was not a gossip or a critic, who was a soul winner.

Several months later Carol Frye Tudor was invited to speak at a teen girls retreat. After church on Sunday night, Kris Matthews Grafton and Jane began asking Carol questions. She kept quoting Mrs. Evans in her answers, which the Holy Spirit used to give Jane a desire to attend Hyles-Anderson College to take Mrs. Evans' classes.

In 1978, after taking classes for one year, Jane was hired to be the secretary to the dean of men and also to be a dormitory supervisor under Mrs. Evans, the dean of women.

Jane was married to Tom Grafton in July of 1982. When their daughter Carissa was born in 1986, Jane began working part-time for Christian Womanhood at home. In 1991 when Carissa entered school, Jane began working in the Christian Womanhood office.

In 2005 Dr. and Mrs. Schaap asked Jane to be the managing editor of Christian Womanhood.

Making Life Happen!

Section 1
Mind Control

"We are what we think,
and we are in the process of becoming what we think."

– Marlene Evans

Just Another Sunday
by Ruby Velez

June 25, 2006, started out as just another Sunday morning. Little did I know that by 1:25 that afternoon, my life would be changed completely.

My family and I arrived at church. My parents had come to visit from Michigan, and we were planning on leaving right after the morning service. Our five-year-old Eliana was so excited to go to Sunday school, and our three-year-old Ricky was just as excited to see his little friends in his class.

As was our routine, I took our four-month-old baby, Damaris Maria, to her nursery. It was her second time in the middler nursery. I had just bought the baby a brand-new Children's Place dress, and I was so proud of it. It only cost $3.98! What a great deal! She looked so very pretty in pink.

After the morning service was over, I went to the nursery to pick up Damaris. As I was talking to two other mothers at the nursery desk—all of us waiting for our babies—we all watched as a security guard rushed into the nursery. Moments later, the emergency response team from our church also rushed into the nursery. I walked over to the window of the nursery to see if I could see Damaris. I looked at the swings and didn't see her. I looked in the cribs and didn't see her. A minute or two later, the EMTs arrived. Not even knowing for sure if my baby was the one who was in trouble, I called my husband on his cell phone and told him to come to the nursery right away. I then looked over to the wall that separated the playroom from the changing station. I saw Linda Ault, the superintendent of that nursery, talking to one of the emergency personnel while going through a black diaper bag that was around her shoulder. I then saw the yellow bottle that I had prepared that morning for Damaris in the side of that diaper bag. I then knew that Damaris was the baby being worked on behind that little wall. As I stood there, I remember feeling an incredible physical presence of peace and calmness. I know now that the Lord Jesus was ever present.

Clyde Wolfe, the chief of security at First Baptist Church, and Linda Ault came and told me that my little Damaris was in trouble. They had found her in her crib not breathing. Only a few short minutes had passed between the time a worker had placed her in the crib and when she was discovered not breathing.

I then saw the EMT rush out of the nursery with Damaris in his arm, giving her mouth-to-mouth resuscitation. I was given instructions to follow him to the waiting ambulance. I jumped into the front seat of that ambulance. I could not pray at the moment, nor could I cry. All that came from my mouth was Bible verses I had memorized. "Saturate your mind with Scripture" is what I had learned from Marlene Evans when I was a student at Hyles-Anderson College. Little did I realize as a young student in her class that her time-released teaching would be a vital life tool for me. On purpose, I turned around in my seat to watch five grown men work intently on Damaris. I didn't want to miss a thing. As she lay there on that bed, her two little pigtails were bouncing up and down from the fervency of those dear medical people who were doing everything humanly possible to start the beating of her little heart. I now know God's will was already done.

The ambulance rushed to St. Margaret's Hospital, the hospital in which Damaris was born. We went into the emergency room where 10 to 15 medical people had already started to work on her. Tubes and wires were everywhere on her lifeless body. I held one of her hands as the team worked on her. Another 10 to 15 people were waiting for their cue to start working on her. I sang "Jesus

Loves Me" and "Jesus Loves the Little Children" to her. A tremendous calmness filled the room. Jesus, I know, was there. The doctors were giving her a strong medication to get her heart beating. Every member of the team was intently performing his job. One of the doctors was giving her a shot in her leg while flicking her foot and saying, "Come on, baby, breathe. Come on, baby, breathe." Everyone wanted Damaris to start breathing. I was crying, of course, but not out of control. I knew that Someone else was in control.

Our Sunday school teacher and his wife, Dr. and Mrs. Bob Marshall, arrived at the hospital moments after we did. The doctor came to tell Rick and me that the situation did not look good. Forty-five minutes had already passed since our sweet baby had first received medical attention. By this time, Pastor and Mrs. Schaap had arrived at the hospital to be with us. Brother Schaap went to Damaris, laid his hand on her head, and began to pray. As he started his prayer with "Father, You are not on trial," a holy hush and an indescribable spirit of peace fell on the emergency room. He went on to say that we would love to keep Damaris, but we wanted His will, not ours. My husband then took Damaris' hand, kissed it, and kissed her forehead. As I stood by the wall watching, I quietly sang "Amazing Grace," and how amazing His grace was for us that day. Rick had me hold her hand again, and I talked into her ear as the nurse moved her head closer to my mouth. "Damaris, this is Mommy. If you are with Jesus right now, that is very fine with me. If you're happy with Jesus, that makes me very happy. Ricky, Eliana, Daddy, and I are going to miss you very much though. I am so happy for you."

As I talked with Damaris, tearful-eyed nurses watched intently—about to lose their composure. The doctor then came to Rick and me and told us that he and his team would have to stop working on her in the next few minutes. Almost 50 minutes had now passed since someone had started working on her to get her to breathe. The few minutes passed, and the team stopped working on our little angel. The doctor checked one more time for a pulse, looked at his wristwatch, then at the clock on the wall, and pronounced her dead. "Now is the will of God," and "Make Christ the center of your life, and the circumference will take care of itself" are what I remembered Dr. Wendell Evans teaching Rick and me when we were college students. I accepted the death of our daughter as the will of God, and the Lord had carried us through the "circumference."

One day while sitting in Mrs. Marlene Evans' Christian Womanhood class as a single college student, she counted four girls sitting in a row. "One, two, three, four…one of you ladies will face cancer or your husband will divorce you," she stated. She counted four more ladies and said, "One of you will have a child die. What will you do then? Will you curse God and die? People, saturate your mind with Scripture and be a different woman." Little did I know what the Lord had planned for me then. How happy I am that I learned that the will of God will bring many hard, painful, and extremely grievous things in our life. But God is so very faithful and good, and through His Word, one can find so much comfort. According to II Corinthians 1:3-5, He is the God of all comfort. *"Blessed be God, even the Father of our Lord Jesus Christ, the Father of mercies, and the God of all comfort; Who comforteth us in all our tribulation, that we may be able to comfort them which are in any trouble, by the comfort wherewith we ourselves are comforted of God. For as the sufferings of Christ abound in us, so our consolation also aboundeth by Christ."*

I remember also when Mrs. Evans said that she was not rejoicing in the fact that she had cancer; she was rejoicing in the fact that there is a Heaven. I cannot humanly rejoice that my sweet daughter is no longer with us, but I am rejoicing that there is a Heaven, that God has allowed us to be in such a tremendous church with such an incredible church family, that the death of my daughter has brought people to Christ, that many new Christians and many marriages have been strengthened by her death, and I could go on and on. I have had to write lists of why I can rejoice through such a huge loss. I have to on purpose keep the right perspective; otherwise, I would just be nervous, worried, and extremely depressed.

As of this writing, we still have not received the official coroner's report for our daughter. What my husband and I have accepted and believe is that her death is absolutely the will of God. This death does not take God by surprise. He had this planned on His calendar long ago. Therefore, He has planned to care for us in a very unique way, and we have sensed His care like never before. Of course, I have many days when I cry a lot and my heart is extremely heavy, but the truth of the aforementioned has brought so much comfort to me personally.

Rick and I have learned so much through the death of our daughter. These lessons may have only come as the result of something like this. How extremely thankful I am for the eternal lessons I learned earlier from Dr. and Mrs. Wendell Evans. Even sweeter is the precious promise of Heaven and the fact that we are children of the King.

1. Saturate your mind with Scripture to prepare for the tough times ahead. Psalm 119:11 says, *"Thy word have I hid in mine heart, that I might not sin against thee."* The Word of God will protect you from responding in a wrong way.

2. When trials and testings come, trust that God has your life in His hands and He is in control. Realize that **nothing** surprises God! Jeremiah 29:11 says, *"For I know the thoughts that I think toward you, saith the Lord, thoughts of peace, and not of evil, to give you an expected end."*

3. Rejoice in those things that heartache, trials, and grief cannot take away.
   - Rejoice that you are saved and on your way to Heaven.
   - Rejoice that there is a Heaven where one day all tears will be wiped away.
   - Rejoice that God wants to use your heartache to make a difference for eternity.
   - Rejoice that no matter what trials come your way, you have the presence of God. Hebrews 13:5b says, *"...for he hath said, I will never leave thee, nor forsake thee."*

Rick Velez and Ruby Saldana met at Hyles-Anderson College. Ruby came under the influence of Marlene Evans in her classes. The young engaged couple sought counsel from the Evanses throughout their engagement. Rick counseled with Dr. Evans, and Ruby counseled with Mrs. Evans. They were married in 1997. After graduating, Ruby taught briefly at Hyles-Anderson College. Both Rick and Ruby are active members of First Baptist Church of Hammond, Indiana. Rick is on the deacon board at First Baptist Church. They are very involved in their adult Sunday school class and serve as discipleship leaders under Dr. Bob Marshall, an assistant pastor at First Baptist Church of Hammond.

Mrs. Evans Said...And I Knew What to Do

by Zana Reichen

At this writing it has been five days since our pastor, Dr. Jack Schaap, announced in church that two of our church members, Rick and Ruby Velez, had lost their four-month-old baby, Damaris. Rick and Ruby are two of our finest. They both graduated from Hyles-Anderson College and are faithful members at First Baptist Church of Hammond. The Homegoing of their precious little girl was unexpected.

I went to Ruby after church Wednesday night to share my condolences with her. I hugged her neck and cried, saying, "I'm so sorry."

She responded with such grace. "Miss Reichen, you wouldn't believe it! As soon as Damaris passed away, I remembered Mrs. Marlene Evans' saying to us in class, *'Rejoice in the Lord alway: and again I say, Rejoice.'* I can rejoice because my baby is in Heaven. I remember her saying to us as she pointed to a row of us girls in college, 'Girls, one day one of you is going to get cancer. One of you is going to lose a baby. What are you going to do then? You must learn to rejoice in the Lord when those times come.' "

I listened to Ruby mesmerized. I listened to her with admiration. She was very intense as she shared these words with me. I told her she was truly a picture of God's grace, and she too gave God the glory for the grace He was supplying.

For you readers who attended Hyles-Anderson College, you are likely picturing a class about to be dismissed by Marlene

Evans—she would not let us go until we all quoted together, "*Rejoice in the Lord alway, and again I say, Rejoice.*" Then, for those of you who were students during her years of chemo, back pain, and other health problems, we witnessed her **live** that very truth—"*Rejoice in the Lord alway....*"

Another thing Mrs. Evans used to say was, "The truths and principles you learn in college are like time-released teaching. You may not need it now, and you may think you forgot what you learned, but years into the future, at the moment you need it, God will bring it to mind." Ruby remembered what she had learned several years before and experienced the "time-released teaching" of Mrs. Evans—just like she said we would.

Mrs. Evans has been in Heaven since 2001, but she "*...being dead yet speaketh,*" and the words she spoke are God's words, so they are everlasting.

Thank you, Mrs. Evans. Though you no longer reside on earth, you are **still** helping ladies!

Trials and tests will come into your life. Be prepared.

1. Learn all you can learn right now. Be faithful to Sunday school and church. Really tune in and listen to the teaching and preaching.
2. Refuse to allow yourself to think, "This doesn't apply to me," when listening to a sermon. Even if you never experience that trial, you will know someone who needs the teaching you are hearing.
3. Read books and listen to speaking and teaching recordings to help you learn all you can learn.
4. Ask the Holy Spirit to help you each day to remember the teachings and Scriptures you have learned that you need that day.

5. Responding in a Christlike manner to the trials of life is a testimony of the grace of God in a person's life—and helps us to influence others for eternity.

In September of 1980 Zana Reichen enrolled as a student at Hyles-Anderson College and came under the influence of Marlene Evans as a teacher. After graduation she became a dormitory supervisor and worked with Mrs. Evans who was the dean of women of Hyles-Anderson College. Zana attended weekly meetings with Mrs. Evans as she taught how to work with the dormitory students.

Life Ain't Fair
by Leslie Beaman

$\mathcal{I}$ have never been much of a "date" person. What I mean by that is I can clearly recall defining moments in my life, but I am not the greatest at remembering the date those moments took place. I will never forget the moment I became a mother for the first time. After years of disappointments (four miscarriages) and much prayer, my husband laughs because though I know my boys' birthdays, I can never remember the year they were born. I can never remember if I was married September 12, 1981, or September 12, 1982, although I remember almost every little detail about my wedding day. (I just checked; it's 1981!) I don't remember the year my mom died, but I know my life was definitely changed after she left us.

I have had many defining moments in my life—moments from which I have walked away changed. I cannot tell you the date, but without a doubt, one such moment was the day I was called from Mayo Clinic and told for the second time Mrs. Evans had cancer. She had already survived breast cancer for 12 years. I remember at the time thinking she only had a few short days left to live. Thankfully, she lived for seven and one-half years after her second diagnosis.

The first time I talked with her after I received the news, I remember saying, "Mrs. Evans, this seems so unfair. I mean, why you?"

I remember her reply. "Leslie, why not me? No one is exempt from heartache. I know life doesn't always seem fair, but God is a just God, and He's the One in control. So even though we don't understand why now, we must trust our good and just Lord that when we get to Heaven, He'll make all things clear." From that day on, I never again said, "This is so unfair" or "Why you?" though I must admit I prayed and cried to the Lord every chance I got.

From time to time my boys have come home from school and said, "This isn't fair," or "That isn't fair," or "He isn't fair," or "She isn't fair." I have always responded, "I'm sorry, Son. Life isn't fair. The most qualified person doesn't always get the job. The hardest worker doesn't always get the bonus. The person who does the most work doesn't always get the most credit."

I have known of people who have worked nonstop for days in their office during a crisis time only to have their boss, who did little to nothing in the way of help, take credit for all the work that transpired. It's painful; it hurts; and yes, it doesn't seem fair. Sadly, we live in a sinful world where people lie and cheat and where we are sometimes totally misunderstood. We have to get beyond the "fair" issue.

Why don't we just be honest? What we are actually saying is "I deserve better. I deserve a bonus. I deserve the award. I deserved to be treated with respect. It's all about "I," "I," "I", "Me," "Me," "Me," "My child," "My husband," and on and on it goes.

This all may be true, but stop keeping score! You will never get what you deserve. We deserve Hell, but thank the Lord, we don't have to go there. I for one am very thankful for that! Praise the Lord!

No, life is not fair, and as hurtful as that may be, you cannot dwell on the negative side of that. Sometimes it seems like good people die young and evil people live forever. But I watched Mrs. Evans' life, and her words still ring in my head: "God is a just God, and He's the one in control. Someday He will make all things clear." So for now, we must trust Him.

"Although the fig tree shall not blossom, neither shall the fruit be in

the vines; the labor of the olive shall fail, and the fields shall yield no meat; the flock shall be cut off from the fold, and there shall be no herd in the stalls: Yet I will rejoice in the LORD, I will joy in the God of my salvation." (Habakkuk 3:17, 18)

Bad things happen to good people. Life isn't always fair. Let's focus on the things we know and the things we can control.

1. Matthew 5:45 reminds us that life is not always fair: *"That ye may be the children of your Father which is in heaven: for he maketh his sun to rise on the evil and on the good, and sendeth rain on the just and on the unjust."*

2. Regardless of how unfair and unjust life may seem, we serve a just and fair God who is good to us. Psalm 73:1 says, *"Truly God is good to Israel, even to such as are of a clean heart."* The important factor is that we keep our heart right through the good times and the tough times.

3. God sends events into our lives to make us better Christians. We should view these events as opportunities to grow in grace rather than an injustice. Job gave us a proper view of life's injustices and difficulties in Job 23:10 when he said of God, *"But he knoweth the way that I take: when he hath tried me, I shall come forth as gold."*

4. Trusting God in the difficult times requires faith. Hebrews 11:6 says, *"But without faith it is impossible to please him: for he that cometh to God must believe that he is, and that he is a rewarder of them that diligently seek him."*

5. God is in control; He is not only aware of every event in your life, but He plans each event. He wants to help you "grow your faith." The apostles said to Jesus in Luke 17:5b, *"...Lord, Increase our faith."*

In 1973 Leslie Simpson Beaman enrolled in Hyles-Anderson College and was immediately captivated by the personality and teaching of Marlene Evans. After graduation, Leslie served on the staff of Hyles-Anderson College with the activities department.

Leslie now serves as a faculty member of the State Line Christian School in Temperance, Michigan. Leslie was greatly used of God in the production and publication of many of Marlene Evans' books. Those of us who benefit from those books owe Leslie a great debt of gratitude.

Marlene Evans
& Leslie Beaman

Crippled With Fear
by Leslie Beaman

It seems like wherever you go, you can't help being bombarded with discouraging news. Interest rates are up, gas prices have soared, unemployment is on the rise, and on and on it goes. I believe now more than ever that we need to suck the joy out of the little things in life that the Lord gives us freely each and every day.

I can picture Mrs. Marlene Evans laughing out loud as if she didn't have a care in the world all the way up until cancer took her life. How could that be? She learned early on how to suck the joy out of life. I heard her say on several different occasions, "Leslie, don't let anyone or anything steal your joy." Mrs. Evans used to call it "mind control." She used to control what her mind dwelled on.

When you feel like life's burdens are closing in on you, dwell on the good things—go for a walk in the park; take a coffee... (I added the coffee part. Ha! Mrs. Evans wouldn't have said that!), sit on a bench and watch the birds or read a book; take a group of preschoolers out for an ice cream cone; listen to a good CD; have a "stupid-joke-fest" day with your teenager; walk along a beach; make a snowman. (You can make a snowman nine months out of the year up north! Ha!) You better learn how to enjoy life's journey, or you're in for a very bumpy ride. Don't allow fear to cripple you.

As a teacher in Christian schools since 1978, I've watched a lot of parents talk their children out of Christian work because they feared their children would have to struggle financially someday. Fear is a crippling thing that will rob you and your family of true happiness.

Let's learn from Marlene Evans to insulate our lives with the Bible and have the Lord help with mind control.

The following is a passage of Scripture Mrs. Evans really loved: *"Rejoice in the Lord alway: and again I say, Rejoice. Let your moderation be known unto all men. The Lord is at hand. Be careful for nothing; but in every thing by prayer and supplication with thanksgiving let your requests be made known unto God. And the peace of God, which passeth all understanding, shall keep your hearts and minds through Christ Jesus. Finally, brethren, whatsoever things are true, whatsoever things are honest, whatsoever things are just, whatsoever things are pure, whatsoever things are lovely, whatsoever things are of good report; if there be any virtue, and if there be any praise, think on these things."* (Philippians 4:4-8)

1. Fill your mind with Bible verses by memorizing Scripture to help when you struggle with wrong thinking.
2. Dwell on positive events and positive people. Refuse to allow negative thoughts to control you.
3. The best way to have right thinking is to practice what Marlene Evans called "substitute thinking." Rather than allowing yourself to think thoughts such as, "I shouldn't be thinking these negative (or fearful or whatever wrong) thoughts," simply bring in the right thoughts. Substituting Bible-taught thoughts or Scripture for the wrong thoughts will drive them out.
4. Use Philippians 4:8 as your guide for your thought life, *"Finally, brethren, whatsoever things are true, whatsoever things are honest, whatsoever things are just, whatsoever things are pure, whatsoever things are lovely, whatsoever things are of good report; if there be any virtue, and if there be any praise, think on these things."*

How to Get Over Your Hurts Fast
by Loretta Walker

During my first year at Hyles-Anderson College, I sat in Marlene Evans' class hearing teaching about being a different woman. While there, I was nursing a bitter spirit concerning relationships of the past. I had been treated unfairly by some people and lived with unforgiveness for those hurts. At this point in my Christian life, I was a Sunday school teacher, a bus worker, a three-to-thrive church attendee, and a person who had daily devotions. Yet, I still allowed a bitter spirit in my life. Of course, I was smart enough not to talk openly to others about these feelings.

However, during Mrs. Evans' classes, the Holy Spirit brought these feelings to the surface. I remember sitting in my seat during a class, confessing my feelings. Many times I had acknowledged the feelings, but I normally made excuses for them rather than admit that they were sin. I believe the admission of my own guilt rather than blaming the fault on the offender was the beginning of getting over my hurts.

I relieved myself of a great burden when I got over the hurt of my past. Mrs. Beverly Hyles said in one of her classes, "Bitterness is the only thing that will eat its own container." Relieve yourself of bitterness and be free!

I would like to share my notes from that class dated September 1978. I trust you will read the points with an open heart. Please receive them if you nurse a bitter spirit or share them with others who need it.

1. **Don't spend time meditating on the hurt of the past.**
Think of the hurts of others. Mrs. Evans had mastered the art of
replacement thinking. She did not say not to think of my hurt—
which is very hard and nearly impossible when you first confess
this bitter spirit. Rather, she said to think of others who have had
greater hurts. "Think on others' thorns and your roses [good
things]" she taught. *"Let this mind be in you, which was also in
Christ Jesus."* (Philippians 2:5) Don't nurse your wound with self-
pity and with thoughts of incrimination toward the one who hurt
you. Instead, look at someone else who has a greater hurt.

2. **Try to find the good that came out of the hurt.** I believe
one of the good things that came out of my hurt is a dependency
on God, which gives me strength. What I mean is that in my need
for a change, I sought God wholeheartedly when I got saved. I
immediately started attending church three times a week. I immediately began reading my Bible daily. I immediately developed a
prayer life. I immediately let my life be centered around God and
the church.

3. **Give the person who has hurt you the benefit of the
doubt.** Mrs. Evans taught, "He did not mean to hurt you. He is
an insecure person. I have no doubt he eventually did feel bad
that he hurt you. He did it because of how he feels about himself."
Mrs. Evans repeatedly told us, "Behavior is always caused, and
causes are always multiple." This thought made me stop to evaluate where the offender learned his behavior. In my case, I remembered the father of the person who hurt me had the same wrong
behavior and had also hurt me on different occasions. This person's drinking habit was because of his insecurity and unhappiness
with life.

When I was a child, I thought he drank because he did not
love me enough to quit. He said and did hurtful things not
because he was out to get me; rather, it was because he really did
not know any better. As an adult, I now realize that the more you

love someone, the more he has the power to hurt you. When we hurt, we take it so personally and feel it was directed at us for the sole purpose of "getting us." In reality, that is not a fact; that is a feeling.

When Loretta Haines Walker was 18 and trying to decide which Christian college to attend, she received a phone call from a lady she had never before met named Marlene Evans. Mrs.

Evans simply asked Loretta if she was going to come to Hyles-Anderson College. Loretta had already decided that whatever college contacted her first would be the college she would attend. Loretta told her "yes." Her first day on campus, she worked in the activities department of which Marlene Evans was in charge. She continued to work for her throughout all of her college days.

Loretta Walker remains a vital Christian Womanhood team member who works with the scheduling and details of booking Christian Womanhood Mini-Spectaculars. Loretta and her husband Kevin and their family crisscross America in the field of evangelism.

My Circle of Protection
by Leslie Beaman

$\mathcal{I}$ used to think that most "drama queens" were teenage girls. As I have grown older, I have realized that a woman of any age can qualify for "drama queendom" (if that is a word).

When I was in my early twenties, I was going through something that I felt was beyond drama and into the area of full-fledged trauma. I had just broken up with someone for whom I cared very deeply; and though I usually don't give way to depression, I was living in one dark pit of despair for weeks. Mrs. Evans came by my office in the Activities Department at Hyles-Anderson College and said, "Leslie, what are you doing tonight? I'd like to take you out to eat."

I was depressed, but I wasn't stupid! I went with her to the Red Lantern Inn, a lovely restaurant overlooking Lake Michigan in the Indiana Dunes. After dinner we went by the waterfront and sat on the beach to talk. I don't remember what she was trying to tell me; I was still stuck in my self-pity mode. I was so self-absorbed that I began to build a stone circle with little pebbles that I found on the beach. After a while I had quite a collection of rocks.

It was then that Mrs. Evans spoke to me in a very stern voice and said, "Leslie, LISTEN TO ME!" She picked up a large stone and placed it in the middle of my circle of stones and said, "This represents you." She added that all the little stones around the big stone were my circle of protection. She said, "Leslie, just pretend these little stones represent your family, friends, the Bible, nature, health—everything good in your life—everything that makes you who you are. Let's take one stone away from your circle of protection." She picked up one stone and threw it in the lake. I looked down and realized it was hard to tell that a stone was even missing. I suddenly realized that what she was trying to say was that I have so many things in my life, why in the world was I so depressed? Why was I ignoring all the good in my life and focusing on one heartache? Suddenly I felt so very small and very stupid. I looked at her and said, "Do you always have to use visual aids when you are teaching me?"

She laughed and said, "Whatever it takes!"

Twenty-seven years later, I am still reminding myself daily to focus on all that God has given to me and everything good in my life, rather than life's losses. Mrs. Evans was trying to prepare me for the hard times. I am still thanking God for Mrs. Evans and for my circle of protection.

It is important to build a circle of protection to help prepare for the difficult times that will come to your life.

1. Get as many interests as possible so you have many things to enjoy—wildlife, birds, flowers, reading, many kinds of music, cooking, etc.

2. Keep busy. Have a number of different areas where you are active so if you lose one area, you still have other responsibilities.

A Visit From the Preacher
by Linda Stubblefield

During Marlene Evans' recovery time after she underwent cancer surgery in 1994, those of us who worked for her took turns staying with her around the clock. My turn was on a Saturday, and she felt well enough to sit in her fireplace room. We were chatting when the doorbell rang. I went to the front door, opened it, and was startled to see our pastor and his wife, Dr. and Mrs. Jack Hyles! Speechless, I just closed the door in their faces. I went back to where Mrs. Evans was sitting and said, "Preacher and Mrs. Hyles are at the front door."

Dr. & Mrs. Jack Hyles

"What? Help me get ready to see them! Did you leave them standing outside?" I think she made the statement and asked the question in one breath! "Go let them in!"

I went back to the door and invited them in. Mrs. Evans greeted them and said, "Oh, Preacher, I have had a vision of your coming to my fireplace room with Mrs. Hyles. In my mind, I've seen you sitting here and Mrs. Hyles sitting beside you here." She pointed to her loveseat. Preacher and Mrs. Hyles sat right where Mrs. Evans had envisioned them!

I excused myself from the room, but I could hear them talking (and I eavesdropped just a wee bit!). At that time, the Mayo Clinic specialists were not offering Mrs. Evans much hope of recuperating from Stage IV ovarian cancer.

Preacher asked, "Mrs. Evans, are you looking forward to meeting some of the patriarchs of the Bible like Moses, Paul, David, Abraham, and of course Jesus?"

I could not see Mrs. Evans' face, but I could surely imagine what she must have looked like when she replied, "Oh, Preacher, I'm not in any real big hurry to meet them; the folks down here are just fine!"

Preacher tried another tactic: "Well, Marlene, are you looking forward to walking on streets of gold?"

"Preacher," she replied, "I really don't mind these asphalt streets down here—potholes and all! I don't mind driving down them at all!"

One statement Mrs. Evans made over and over as she battled cancer for almost 20 years was, "I'm going to live until I die." Mrs. Evans loved life more than any person I believe I have ever known. She made cancer her friend instead of her enemy. She accepted the negative of cancer; and in true Marlene Evans fashion, made a positive out of an extremely negative situation and wrote three books to help her cancer buddies. She did indeed love life and lived life; to Mrs. Evans, everything was a happening—from going to church to teaching classes to enjoying nature. She kept her mind focused on the positives and good things of life to keep a happy spirit.

One of the greatest temptations for people who are ill, especially those who are suffering from an incurable disease, is to become depressed and focus on themselves, their illness, and the bleak future they are facing.

1. While you are well, develop a positive mind-set so you are in the habit of thinking good thoughts.
2. Right thinking—Philippians 4:8 types of thoughts—is a discipline. It does not just happen. People have right thinking because they discipline themselves to do so.

3. Daily we are practicing for our future. Each day we are becoming more of what we are. If we live a selfish life filled with self pity, negative thinking, and worry, we will grow into selfish, negative old ladies. However, if we discipline our minds, our tongues, and our attitudes, we will grow into delightful, generous, fun older ladies.

4. Each of us chooses our future—not necessarily what events come our way, but how we respond to those events.

Linda Alexander Stubblefield transferred to Hyles-Anderson College in 1974. One of her classes that first semester, Christian Womanhood, was taught by Marlene Evans. Linda began working for Mrs. Evans in 1976 as a student secretary, typing her correspondence.

Linda Stubblefield has worked in various capacities in the ministry of Christian Womanhood since her graduation from Hyles-Anderson College in 1977. At present she serves as the assistant editor.

Right: Linda Stubblefield honors Marlene Evans at her fiftieth birthday party with a gift of words in one of Mrs. Evans' college classes at Hyles-Anderson College.

Chasing the Redbirds
by Leslie Beaman

If I didn't learn anything else from Marlene Evans, the one thing that will forever stick in my head was the fact that she was continually reminding herself and anyone who would listen how good God is. Mrs. Evans used the redbird as a sort of reminder of God's love. Whenever a redbird passed her way, she'd say, "The Lord sent that redbird by this morning to remind me He loves me!"

You'd probably think she was making it up if you didn't know her, but she was continually making statements like, "Look at the sunset God gave us this evening." She loved going for a drive and observing nature. She would often say, "Look at those trees. It's like they're holding hands. I love driving through this tunnel of trees!" I remember once she came over to the ladies' dormitories of Hyles-Anderson College where I lived, had me jump in her car, and without many words, drove like we were going to a fire, only to stop in front of a big, old, strange-looking tree and announce, "Isn't that wonderful? God made that!"

After many years I got used to Mrs. Evans' constantly pointing out all the wonderful ways God shows us that He loves us. It's so hard driving down a street without wanting to call her to say, "I saw a redbird today," or "You should see the wildflowers by my house," or "The sunset last night was that orange coral color you love so much."

I know I've said this before, but it bears repeating. This is the reason Mrs. Evans could be dying and still have her joy intact. She could be on chemotherapy treatments and still smile when a red-bird flew by the window of her car or laugh at two squirrels playing in a tree. She surrounded herself with the Lord's love whenever life's trials threatened to slap her down.

Now I don't think I could ever be or hope to be the Christian testimony Mrs. Evans was. But yesterday as I sat waiting for my son's basketball practice to get over (it was running late, and I was tired of waiting), a redbird landed on the hood of my car. I said, "Okay, I see it, Mrs. Evans."

God loves me! Is He real to you?

Life's Changes
by Leslie Beaman

When I was growing up, two weeks of every summer of my life was spent at my grandparents' house in Canada. My grandparents, Marie and Henry Bechard, were Canadians who owned a two-bedroom cottage on a large piece of land on Lake St. Clair in Belle River, Canada. I loved those weeks with my grandparents. They were "magical." We swam, fished, took walks to the nearby lighthouse, and watched the big boats sail right by from the living room of my grandparents' home. Needless to say, when my grandparents passed away, I did not want to revisit the cottage I had loved so much. I never liked change much, and I knew if I revisited the cottage with its new owners now taking up residence, I would have to come to the stark realization that a special part of my life was now over.

I know this all sounds childish, but the above paragraph is the same reason why I did not want to read the *Christian Womanhood* magazine after Marlene Evans passed away. I did not want to be reminded that she was no longer alive and contributing to the ladies' paper for which she had such a passion. Then one day someone handed me a copy of the new *Christian Womanhood*. I felt very guilty as I had to admit that the new paper/magazine was quite good. It was now in color, shiny, pretty, and packaged in a way that anyone would have to sit up and take notice.

Then I thought, "Okay, it's packaged in a first-class way, but what about the content?"

I found myself studying the new (so-called) *Christian Womanhood* with a negative spirit, and again I had to admit it was very well done! It's powerful, passionate, exciting, and motivational. It is everything Mrs. Evans would have loved. It was then I realized that if you really care for someone you would want that person's life work to continue and succeed long after his/her death. Mrs. Evans would have been brokenhearted if the things into which she had put her heart and soul had diminished so quickly.

I love *Christian Womanhood* because of what it stands for, and also because it is a monthly reminder that Mrs. Evans' memory is still alive and well. It is a reminder that a part of the woman I loved so much wasn't lost when she went to be with the Lord.

I know First Baptist Church of Hammond, Indiana, has changed since Dr. Hyles' death. Change is inevitable. I also know Brother Hyles would be thrilled beyond words to know his life's work for the Lord is flourishing and successful in such a wonderful way long after his death. What a wonderful tribute to a person's memory.

For the most part, change is a part of life. To avoid change would be to avoid living. On the other hand, we need to take all we can from the past and carry it into the future lest we forget the great contributions of people like Mrs. Marlene Evans and Dr. Jack Hyles.

I heard Dr. Hyles once say, "Gratitude has a short memory." Unfortunately, I've found that the statement is true, and I am determined to change that in my life. I thank the Lord daily for godly people like Dr. Hyles and Mrs. Evans who have invested so much in my life. I am grateful beyond words, and I plan on shouting it loud and clear to anyone who will listen for the rest of my life. No! Gratitude does not have to have a short memory.

Thanks for Listening
by Zana Reichen

You are talking to a friend or a relative. You are spilling your guts. You are opening your heart and soul to someone you trust or want to confide in while that person is supposedly listening as he or she is straightening the desk, cooking, looking through a book, or walking around doing some other physical thing. About every 20 seconds, the person will say, "Uh-huh," or "Right," or "Okay," and you are thinking to yourself, "Are you really listening to me?" You never quite know for sure if the person is listening other than his occasional "Uh-huh."

I never had to wonder if Marlene Evans was listening to me. She didn't just listen with her ears. She listened with her eyes. She listened with her facial expressions. She listened with her body affixed in a position toward me. She listened with her heart, and she listened with her mind. Mrs. Evans had a unique ability to make people feel important, and I believe one of her top ways was she listened whenever anyone of any age, color, or walk of life talked to her.

A story was told to me that a lady walked up to Mrs. Evans to share a burden. The lady was not dressed in a modest fashion. After the lady left, a person nearby commented to Mrs. Evans about how the lady was dressed, and Mrs. Evans said, "I didn't notice." How typical of Marlene Evans! She kept her eyes fixed on the eyes of the person talking to her. She didn't judge her by her apparel. She listened to this dear lady's burden and made her feel loved and important.

Whenever I talked to Mrs. Evans, she responded with a nod of her head. She responded with appropriate and well-chosen words that assured me she was catching everything I said. She allowed me to say everything I wanted to say, without interruption, before offering solutions.

Mrs. Evans made an art out of listening. She listened to children. She listened to co-workers. She listened intently to her husband. (I witnessed this numerous times!) She listened to the elderly. She just listened to everyone because everyone was important to her! I admired Mrs. Evans for this trait because those of us who knew her, knew she loved to talk; yet when there was a need to listen, she listened. What balance!

Thanks for listening!

The following are seven statements about listening that I learned from Mrs. Evans.

1. Listening makes a person feel loved and important.
2. Listening is not interrupting when a person is sharing her burden.
3. Listening is more than being in the same room with a person when the person is talking.
4. Effective listening is sitting still, focusing on the person, and doing no other physical thing while he or she is talking to you.
5. Listening is therapeutic to the talker.
6. Listening takes time, and people are worth the time.
7. Listening may not always entail a solution from the listener—just sometimes a listening ear.

My View From the Ditch

by Leslie Beaman

While I worked in the Activities Department at Hyles-Anderson College, we had an unwritten rule concerning activities. "Do it fast, do it cheap, don't make waves, and don't forget to clean up before the process starts over again." I remember one particular activity on which I was working during my second year on staff. We were having a kind of a country festival in the student lobby. One of my reluctant friends was talked into bringing a baby calf to the school in the backseat of his Volkswagen Beetle (I didn't say we were smart). Carol Frye Tudor, Bill McSpadden, Jerry Scott, and I were all running around getting things ready. We had haystacks, farm animals, music, and apple cider. I cannot remember much more about it except it was a lot of fun.

The morning before the activity, I had Mrs. Evans' car, and I was driving on the back roads near the college. I don't recall being in much of a hurry, but I do remember thinking Mrs. Evans would need her car soon, and I did not want her to wait on me. I still had a few more items to pick up for the evening's activity. As I rounded a corner, I could hardly believe my eyes. Two cars were driving right toward me, and one of them was in my lane. I don't know if they were racing or if the one car was trying to pass the other on the narrow two-lane road.

I didn't have much time to react, so I slammed on my brakes and my car skidded into a deep ditch. The person driving the car in my lane also slammed on his brakes. When he realized what he had done and saw my car wedged in the ditch, he took off. A man I believed at the time was a farmer came running over to where I was and said, "I saw the entire thing, and that guy almost killed you. If you had stayed on the road, you'd be dead."

I couldn't get the door open on the car, so I had to crawl out the driver's side window. I was glad to be alive until I got a good look at Mrs. Evans' car. It was then that living didn't seem so appealing. Her car was totally wrecked.

The man who had helped me ran to his house and phoned the college. I was sitting on the hood of the car pretty shaken up when two co-workers, Bill McSpadden and Jerry Scott, showed up. They took one look at the car and said, "It really looks bad."

The car had to be pulled out and towed to the nearest station. I remember asking Bill what he thought Mrs. Evans would say. He said he didn't know, but he went on to say he was surely glad he wasn't the one driving!

The man who had helped me wasn't able to get the license plate number of the other car. I cannot tell you in words how sick I felt. When I got to the campus, I went to Mrs. Evans' office. I walked really slow. I felt like the Tin Man going before the great and powerful Oz.

When I walked into her office, she asked, "How are you?"

All I could say was, "I'm so sorry."

She cut me off and said, "Are you hurt?"

I was sore, but I would be fine; her car was another story.

Mrs. Evans looked me in the eyes and said, "People are more important than things. The car can be fixed. Are you sure you're okay?"

I was stunned. Where did this woman come from—Mars? I mean, who talks like that? I just smashed up her car, and she wanted to know how I was feeling?! I believe her response shook me up more than the accident did.

Could it be that this is the way Christians are supposed to respond to problems? I couldn't help but love this lady. She taught me more by example than I would ever learn from any textbook or college class. Mrs. Evans' priority was always people.

Dealing with people in everyday life is an amazing privilege. When we face problems and difficulties with other people, we should always remember to have a Christlike attitude.

1. Keep in mind that people are more important than things.
2. Our reactions to tough times and hard situations have a lot to do with the outcome. God has given us great power in our words, and oftentimes we can make or break a situation with our words and reactions alone.
3. A wise man once said, "Hold very loosely onto the things of this world." Matthew 24:35a says, *"Heaven and earth shall pass away...."* Only things eternal really matter.
4. This does not mean we should be careless and not care for the things God has given us; we simply need to keep them in proper perspective.

Mrs. Evans listened attentively to Pastor Billy Welch. This picture illustrates her ability to block out everything and everyone else to give her complete attention to the person with whom she was conversing.

Her Silence Spoke Volumes— During Critical Times

by Leslie Beaman

$\mathcal{I}$ remember the day I was to meet with Marlene Evans and several of her friends in order to discuss the planning of an upcoming event. The mood was light and fun as we gathered at one of Mrs. Evans' top ten restaurants. Of course all the waiters, waitresses, dishwashers, hostesses, managers, and even the delivery people knew Mrs. Evans. After she had greeted everyone in the place by name (a slight exaggeration—she missed some of the patrons), we all sat down.

Almost immediately Mrs. Evans took charge, making sure everyone was comfortable. She made sure everyone had what she wanted or needed. After all the food was ordered, she settled back, and we all began talking. After awhile, I noticed that something was missing. Mrs. Evans wasn't talking—not a word. If you knew Mrs. Evans for more than one day, you would know there were only four or five reasons why she would not be talking:

- She was exhausted. On this particular day, I knew that wasn't the case because Mrs. Evans seemed very rested.
- She was very focused on listening to a preacher, administrator, or teacher. Again, in this particular situation, this was not the case.
- She was pausing so she could be sure to use the right words. (This usually happened when she was counseling someone.) I hoped this was the case.
- She had just asked a question, and she was intently wait-

ing for the answer. This also was not the case as she had not asked anyone anything.

- Someone had said something very wrong. This was the reason I feared the most—Mrs. Evans wasn't speaking because she didn't care for the direction the conversation was headed. Either someone had criticized a leader; someone had criticized a past decision in front of people who could do nothing to fix the problem; or else the group at the table were "cutting" on each other, and the conversation was going far beyond the realm of good, clean fun and running into hurtful, cutting sarcasm.

I really feared that reason number five had caused Mrs. Evans not to speak. If she were with a group of women and she felt she was in charge, she would soon let everyone know how disappointed she was with our talk. If she was in a group and she felt that she was not in charge, she would either suddenly walk out or stay and remain very quiet, depending on the group and situation.

In a matter of a few minutes, Mrs. Evans spoke up and said, "I do not like where this conversation is heading." We had been joking around with each other, and Mrs. Evans was afraid if we continued, someone was going to be hurt by a careless, unkind comment.

Someone at the table piped up with, "Mrs. Evans, we were just joking." I nodded in agreement.

Mrs. Evans flashed a look at me that no one could misinterpret and said, "I hate joking when it's at someone else's expense. I love to have fun as much as the rest of you, but I won't hurt anyone as a result of that fun."

Mrs. Evans had a way of sensing where a conversation was heading before it ever hit a "gray" area. Through the years I listened to Mrs. Evans and learned a lot. I also learned to listen for her silent moments—for they spoke volumes too.

Mrs. Evans was always careful to watch how words affected people. She knew our words have incredible power—the power to help someone greatly or hurt someone deeply.

1. Be conscious of your words. Don't let "joking around" turn into something hurtful, mean, negative, or critical.

2. Think before you speak! Realize that the words you say may actually hurt someone, even if that person is laughing on the outside. Oftentimes people laugh to save face while they are hiding their true feelings.

3. Be a fun person but be sure never to have fun at someone else's expense.

4. Remember Proverbs 18:21, *"Death and life are in the power of the tongue: and they that love it shall eat the fruit thereof."*

A Southern Belle Wannabe

by Leslie Beaman

At the beginning of my third year at Hyles-Anderson College, a young pastoral student came into one of my Bible classes and said, "Hey, does anyone want to write a few letters to an older, retired pastor?" He went on to explain that this certain pastor was really a great preacher in his time, but his wife had passed away, and he really did not preach very often anymore. Many of the students in the class recognized that elderly pastor's name, but I, having been a Christian a grand total of three years, had never heard of the man. This was no surprise since the first time I had heard of one of my heroes, Dr. Jack Hyles, was a few months before I attended Hyles-Anderson College.

I took the elderly preacher's address and started writing him letters. I really can't tell you why I wrote the letters I did. I remember feeling very lonely at the time. Within weeks this elderly preacher began writing back to me. He really had an unbelievable way of expressing himself. His letters were so kind and encouraging; I thought maybe he was a bit lonely too.

Some time passed, and I heard Brother Hyles make the announcement that he had invited a preacher by the name of Dr. R. G. Lee to come and speak at the college and the church. Dr. Lee was to preach his famous sermon "Pay Day Someday." Brother Hyles went on to describe Dr. Lee as a "preacher's preacher," a "pulpit giant," and a "legend in his own time."

I remember thinking, "Could that Dr. R. G. Lee be the same elderly preacher I have been writing all this time?" It didn't take long before I was informed that the Dr. Lee I had been writing was the same Dr. Lee who would be coming to the college!

I am not sure how everything fell into place, but before I knew it, Carol Frye Tudor, who was in charge of the college Activities Department at the time, told Mrs. Evans about my letters to Dr. Lee. Mrs. Tudor talked with me and told me that in order to

honor Dr. Lee, they wanted me to speak on behalf of the student body and welcome him to the college. I felt sick! And I mean sick! Dr. Lee was from the South, and they wanted me to wear a Southern belle dress, hoop skirt, and all the regalia.

Now mind you, I really wanted to meet Dr. Lee, but the thought of the Southern belle dress with a hoop skirt in front of the entire student body really made me more than uncomfortable. Being reared with three brothers, I've always felt much more

Leslie presents a gift box to R. G. Lee

comfortable playing football in the backyard than I ever did playing dolls with friends.

I ran to Mrs. Evans in a total panic. "I am **not** the Southern belle type," I moaned. "I **can't** do this!"

With a smirk she said, "You can do this! No one else knows how uncomfortable you feel, and if you don't tell them, they will never know. Leslie, stop thinking about how **you** feel and concentrate on how you can best honor Dr. Lee."

If Mrs. Evans were here today, she would probably be saying, "It's not all about you! Get over it!" (Ha!)

Sometimes our feelings and preferences need to be put aside in order to help someone else. Remember a few principles when those events occur:

1. It's not all about you! It is all about letting the name of Jesus be glorified through you.
2. The fact is, we cannot do the things we need to do—in our own strength. But we have the promise of Philippians 4:13 which says, *"I can do all things through Christ which strengtheneth me."*
3. No one will know how uncomfortable you are in a situation unless you let that person know. Ask Jesus for the power to humble yourself and do the right thing.
4. Just because something doesn't sound like fun, it doesn't mean it won't be! Give it a try. Making someone else feel better will be more enjoyable than you think—I promise!

Making Life Happen!

Section 2
Building Happy Relationships

"*L*ove people and like things.
Don't love things and like people."

– Marlene Evans

Woman the Adjuster

by Loretta Walker

Many years ago Marlene Evans gave a talk entitled "Telling Your Husband What You Need." In that talk, she explained how a wife needs to communicate to her husband without complaining or sounding critical toward him.

This talk made me think I could talk to Mrs. Evans about something that I felt needed to be fixed in my marriage relationship. I decided to ask her how to talk to Kevin about something with which I had a difficult time. My problem was, I did not like any public show of affection. I felt embarrassed to have a "liplock" in front of my own children. I felt funny when he would hug me in front of teenagers. I thought when I asked Mrs. Evans what to do about this situation, she would explain to me how to ask Kevin to quit doing it or explain to him that I was uncomfortable. Boy, was I ever in for a shock!

She simply said, "Loretta, you just need to get over feeling funny about it! I think the best way for you to get over it would be to instigate this affection." That is not what I wanted to hear! I wanted her to tell me how to tell Kevin what I needed him to do; instead, she thought that I was the one who needed to change. After I got over the initial shock of her solution to my problem, I said, "Okay, if that is what I need to do, that is what I will do."

After that weekend, I went home to Kevin a new woman. As I recall, we were to leave as soon as I walked in the door. So the kids piled in the back seat, and I got in the front passenger seat. No sooner had Kevin sat down and put the vehicle in gear, than I reached over and squeezed his leg, leaned over, and kissed his cheek. He looked at me like I had grown another head! The poor man was so shocked he almost hit a tree on the way off the mountain! (We lived at the top of a mountain in West Virginia.)

I laughed and thus began my "more affectionate in public" program. When I say more affectionate, I am not talking about laying all over each other or making out in a public place. I'm talking about grabbing his hand, putting my arm through his, a simple peck, or playful pats. I used to believe that in most situations the other person was supposed to understand me and adjust to me. Mrs. Evans felt, and I believe the Bible teaches, that in order to be a different woman, a woman used of God, you are to be the one who adjusts.

1. Genesis chapter one tells that God created Adam, the first man. From Adam, God created Eve, the first woman. Genesis 2:18 states, *"And the LORD God said, It is not good that the man should be alone; I will make him an help meet for him."* Those two words, *help meet* mean "a helper that is suitable" for him.

2. A wife's purpose is to be what her husband needs. You don't have to be what Kevin Walker needs you to be. You are to be what your husband needs. *"Neither was the man created for the woman; but the woman for the man."* (I Corinthians 11:9)

3. Study your husband to learn what he needs from you.

4. Keep in mind that one of the greatest needs a man has from his wife is respect. Ephesians 5:33 says, *"Nevertheless let every one of you in particular so love his wife even as himself; and the wife see that she reverence her husband."* To reverence means to respect. The greatest thing you can do for your husband is to fulfill that need to be respected.

5. It is also important to seek counsel from someone who will tell you what you need to hear and not just what you want to hear. A wise woman will seek wise counsel and then put into the practice the counsel she received.

"I Speak Simpson"
by Leslie Beaman

While I was in high school, I signed up for French as it was the foreign language I most wanted to learn. My grandparents were French Canadian, and so there are some differences in the way I learned to speak French in school and the way they spoke French. Still, I thought they'd love to hear their grandchild speaking their language. (My grandparents also spoke English.)

Besides a few words and phrases, it's hard to tell I studied the language at all. I really learned more from my grandparents than I ever did in the classroom. It's funny. Though I never quite mastered the French language, I do speak several foreign languages. For one, I speak "Simpson" very well. "Simpson" is my maiden name. If you know my family, you know we have a language all our own. Let me share a few examples:

Once when I was 10 or 12 years of age, my parents were planning on going out to dinner with several other couples. I can't remember what was so special about this occasion, but my mother was really looking forward to it. With five children at home, the thought of going out for the evening must have been very exciting. Dad had a sad expression on his face when he informed me that they were no longer going out with their friends.

"Why?" I quickly asked.

"I don't know," Dad said. "Your mother just changed her mind and doesn't want to go."

I'm no genius, but nothing Dad had told me made sense. I remember going into my parents' bedroom and looking in my mom's closet. It suddenly dawned on me. "Mom doesn't want to go out because she really doesn't have anything to wear," I thought. Nothing in my mom's closet was fancy enough for this special dinner. I went back to Dad.

"Dad," I said, "I know why Mom doesn't want to go! She does not want to go because she doesn't have anything right to wear."

"How do you know that? Did your mom say something?"

"No," I replied, "but I know I'm right."

Dad must have said something to Mom because the next thing I knew, Mom and I were dress shopping. I even talked her into getting new shoes. I can't tell you how happy I was watching my mom and dad leave the house that evening. It's possibly one of my best memories as a child. No, I don't speak French, but I definitely speak "Simpson."

I remember Dr. Jack Hyles telling a story about having dinner at his mother's house. I can't recall if it was Thanksgiving or another holiday, but Grandma Hyles had invited her son for dinner. A week or so before the dinner, Grandma Hyles called Brother Hyles and said she was going to have to cancel. Brother Hyles knew his mother well enough to know there was more to the story than what she was saying. Brother Hyles worked it out to get some money to his mom, and soon after she received the money, she called Brother Hyles and simply said that she would like to go ahead with the dinner if he could still come. I guess Brother Hyles had mastered the "Hyles" language.

Mrs. Marlene Evans' favorite line (I believe I heard her say it at least 100 times) was "Behavior is caused, and causes are multiple." Many times people say one thing and yet mean something totally different. My mother passed away about six years ago, and my father, in some ways, still hasn't had the easiest time living without her. For one thing, Dad isn't much of a housekeeper. I did not even know if he knew how to turn on the washing machine or dryer until he told me was going to do some wash.

My dad is a "Ward Cleaver" type of guy. He's never worn blue jeans in his entire life—at least I've never seen him in them. He calls tennis shoes "rubber shoes," and he can't understand why men his age wear them. Dad wears button-down shirts with collars wherever he goes. His shirts are always starched and pressed just so. Dad sends his shirts to the cleaners every week because he likes the sharp pressed look only the cleaners seem to get. My dad is a brilliant, soft-spoken (unless you anger him), professional-looking man. I've, of course, known him all my life, and yet I'm just learning his language.

On my birthday, he called and said, "If you'll come up, I'll take ya out for dinner." In "Simpson" that means, "I miss you, and I'm a bit lonely." I went for a visit two days later.

When I visit Dad, I take him wherever he wants to go. He doesn't walk very well, so I grill him for a list of things he needs at the store. Usually, I have to beg him for the list as he never wants "to put me out."

I really listen to Dad talk. If he ever says "I'd like..." or "I need..." or "Thus and so would be nice," I try to get it for him. Now I haven't always been great at reading him. I am getting better at learning his language. It just takes time. Foreign languages always do! Learn to read the signs with your teens, your husband, and your co-workers. Mrs. Evans was so good at this. I pray I will get better.

Learn your family's "language" and become proficient at it. Learn what they really mean when they make statements. In addition to helping you understand people, it will probably spare a lot of hurt feelings, especially if the person speaking tends to make harsh statements.

1. Figuring out what people really mean when they speak will help you be able to give them what they need. Being a "need filler" is a great way to build relationships.

2. The book of Jude explains that you reach and relate to

people in different ways when it says in verses 22 and 23, *"And of some have compassion, making a difference: And others save with fear, pulling them out of the fire; hating even the garment spotted by the flesh."* In other words, different people speak and hear different "languages."

$\mathscr{B}e$ $\mathscr{E}veryone's$ $\mathscr{C}heerleader$

by Zana Reichen

$\mathscr{M}$any of Mrs. Evans' life practices were caught not by sitting under her tutelage but by simply watching the lady day by day or by listening to someone else repeat to others what Mrs. Evans taught. One of those repeaters is my good friend, Mrs. Carol Tudor. Several years ago Mrs. Tudor came into a staff meeting at Hyles-Anderson College one day very excited about a conversation she'd had with Mrs Evans. She said they had made a conscious decision to be everyone's cheerleader. I sat there thinking, "Okay, go on...."

As it happens anywhere and everywhere, be it the secular workplace or the ministry, people can get bogged down with the negatives of the work. That is easy to do, mainly because of our imperfect human nature. Sad to say, some are "caught up" in the negatives of not meeting the expectations of a boss, allowing constructive criticism to overtake their minds, or just listening to criticism of others. The bottom line is we just do not "cheer" each other enough—or so said Mrs. Evans. How was this spectacular lady, Marlene Evans, **everyone's** cheerleader?

1. **She responded positively anytime love or service—big or small—was shown to her.** She didn't just say, "Thank you," with a courtesy smile. I mean, SHE RESPONDED! She made delightful noises. She giggled. She said, "WOW! I love it!" She moved her hands and opened her mouth wide as she gasped in delight. The woman responded positively so that you had NO DOUBT she was pleased. Just her response was a cheer for you.

2. **She spread "good gossip" about people.** She didn't repeat gossip as WE know gossip—the negative. No, if she found

out something good about you or something good you did, the woman was like a wildfire telling people what good she knew!

3. **She lived by her axiom, "I see gold glittering."** Because Mrs. Evans saw good in everyone, she was every person's cheerleader. She searched for the good in everyone, and as soon as she found it, she would tell the person the good quality she saw in him or her. I have seen people grow by leaps and bounds because Mrs. Evans was their cheerleader for this new outstanding quality she had discovered!

4. **Mrs. Evans found a way for people to put their positive quality to good use.** She gave them jobs to do to enhance their quality. She told other leaders about the newfound qualities in people she had discovered so other leaders could use those people and their qualities in the ministry, thus enabling the people to have a greater potential.

5. **Mrs. Evans wrote short positive messages to people.** She wrote the messages on her famous "fat little notebook" paper and sent the notes through the mail. We all love mail—especially when it's good news about us and especially when it comes from someone we admire! She kept that notebook with her at all times. Her thought was that most people don't send thoughtful notes because they don't have the right stationery, etc. She used her Flair pen and a piece of notebook paper, wrote the note, and sent it.

6. **Mrs. Evans was (as the title conveys)** *everyone's* **cheerleader.** She was just as excited about the educable slow child's words as she was about Dr. Jack Hyles' preaching. She was as equally excited about meeting a new friend in an eight-year-old child as she was about spending time with her *Christian Womanhood* staff ladies. She was just as excited about a Chicago bus teenager giving his life to the Lord as she was about serving the girls and ladies at Hyles-Anderson College as the dean of women or in teaching a college class.

Mrs. Evans was by no means a respecter of persons. She was **everyone's** cheerleader. Maybe that is why the lady was surrounded by people everywhere she went. She made people feel good about themselves. Let's be different and decide to be everyone's cheerleader like Mrs. Evans was. HOORAY FOR PEOPLE!

Building Strong Relationships
by Kris Grafton

Thursday morning on July 6, 2001, Loretta Walker and I took Marlene Evans and her oxygen and her wheelchair out to what would be her last breakfast in a restaurant. Mrs. Evans wasn't really interested in eating; she wanted to talk and teach. She expounded on what she called, "interpret it and shovel it." In other words, "interpret" the good someone said or meant and "shovel" that good to the right person for building and encouraging.

Mrs. Evans was excited because she had gotten to "shovel" some building words to Brother Johnny Colsten, the associate pastor of First Baptist Church of Hammond. "It was because of you, Kris!" she exclaimed.

On the drive home from Mayo Clinic the previous week, Mrs. Evans had called her family with the news that the Mayo Clinic doctors had reached the decision that nothing more could be done for her. Sarah Rivera and I had been taking turns driving, and it was my turn to take a break. As I was resting, Mrs. Evans asked me to finish making some phone calls for her.

I had made several away-from-home calls with no problem. Next, I was to call Brother Colsten. When I dialed the Colstens' number, Brother Colsten answered the phone. As soon as I heard his voice, I burst into tears and could hardly talk. I was trying to sob quietly as I gave Brother Colsten the message from Mrs. Evans in as few words as possible.

After I said goodbye, Mrs. Evans turned around and asked me what had happened that made me burst into tears. "Just hearing Brother Colsten's voice as he answered the phone brought me such comfort and reassurance that everything would be all right in the days ahead, I started to cry."

Mrs. Evans "interpreted" my burst of tears as much love and care from Brother Colsten. Then she took the opportunity to "shovel" to Brother Colsten encouraging words of how much compassion he has in his voice.

Mrs. Evans said every relationship in life would be strengthened if we would "interpret it and shovel it."

1. The natural tendency for people is to hear the negative comments people make and remember them, repeat them to others, and focus on those negatives.

2. Mrs. Evans worked against this tendency and was constantly listening for the good people said.

3. One of her biggest thrills was to be able to pass that good information on to others. Doing so did several things and will help us also:

   • It made her a happy, positive person with whom people wanted to spend time.

   • It encouraged other people and reinforced good behavior. She was much quicker to repeat the good someone had done than to point out a mistake he or she had made.

   • In fact, one of her most effective ways of correcting the people who worked for her was to praise them when she saw them doing something right in a problem area.

4. Find delight in listening for good things and then tell it over and over. Talk the good!

Kris Grafton first heard Marlene Evans speak at a Mother-Daughter Banquet in Rosemount, Minnesota, and immediately thought how much she wanted to have the Bible thinking and love for people she saw so evident in Marlene Evans' life. At the time, she was a nurse working in intensive care at the University of Minnesota Hospitals in Minneapolis, Minnesota. Two months later, Carol Frye Tudor visited her church, met Kris, and told her she needed Hyles-Anderson College. Kris resigned her job and came to Hyles-Anderson with the goals of becoming a better Christian and a better soul winner, and later when she married to be a good wife and mother.

Kris first worked as a secretary for two years and then was asked to be the clinic head nurse in 1978 under the direction of Dr. Dennis Streeter. Kris worked under Mrs. Evans' direction for five years as a dormitory supervisor. Because of her belief in the ministry of Christian Womanhood, Kris has always worked in some way for Christian Womanhood—either in a volunteer capacity or as a paid, part-time worker.

The Importance of People
by Jane Grafton

One of the great privileges of the Christian life is getting to know and laboring with some wonderful Christian people. One of those God has brought into my life is Janice Wolfe. Though I have known Janice since she was a dormitory student at Hyles-Anderson College, I am getting to know her in a new way as she now works part-time in Christian Womanhood. She shared an anecdote with me one day that I felt showed both Janice's spirit and one aspect of Marlene Evans' greatness.

I suddenly realized that I had been calling Janice "Jan" all day. I have several friends and loved ones who go by "Jan," and I guess I was doing so out of habit. I said, "I've been calling you 'Jan' today, haven't I?" She said that was fine and was so gracious about my mistake. I then asked, "Does anyone else call you Jan?"

She answered, "The only person who has ever called me Jan was Mrs. Evans. She did so for several years, and one day it must have dawned on her that everyone else called me Janice. She said, 'I've been calling you Jan. Do people ever call you Jan?' "

Mrs. Evans felt that people were important; and therefore, she was very careful to spell names properly, pronounce names properly, and address people by their preferred name—given name, nickname, etc.

Janice, not wanting to embarrass Mrs. Evans and not wanting to correct a leader, quipped, "Only those who love me in a special way."

Until Mrs. Evans' Homegoing, she addressed her as "Jan," letting her know she was loved by this great lady in a special way!

1. Gustave Flaubert (1821-80) is credited with making the statement, "God is in the details—whatever one does should be done thoroughly; details are important."
2. One of the attributes that set Marlene Evans apart in the area of human relationships was the details. She was careful about the details of a relationship. Many people have difficulty remembering names or remembering how to spell someone's name. She never tossed off comments like "Oh, I just have a hard time remembering names" as an excuse for not knowing someone's name. She worked carefully to learn people's names and then remember them. She also was careful to spell their names correctly. She would ask them how to spell their name rather than assume she knew the correct spelling.
3. Caring about details such as names, correct spellings, etc. makes people feel very loved. It makes the statement that the person is important to you. You will make a greater impact on lives for eternity when you care for the details.

I Can't Understand!
by Rena Fish

Before I was married, I had the privilege of working as a dormitory supervisor at Hyles-Anderson College. Mrs. Evans was serving as the dean of women, but her health was to the point that she no longer made it to our weekly "dorm supe" meetings. One week, however, Mrs. Evans was feeling well enough to attend the meeting, and we were privileged to sit under her expert teaching as to how to reach the girls on our dorm floor. She encouraged us to learn the stories behind our girls so that we could better understand the circumstances that had brought them to Hyles-Anderson College and had molded their lives thus far.

As I pondered her words, I began to feel quite inadequate to be able to help my girls. I simply could not fathom what it would be like to live in a drunkard's home or to be afraid of one's own father. I could not even understand the challenges that a girl would face who came to a Christian college after years of public school. It was beyond my comprehension to know what it would be like to have your parents divorce or to have your home church go through a major split while you were in college. My life had included two wonderful parents who kept me in a stable church and a Christian school all of my growing up years.

I was beginning to think that perhaps I was not the right person for the job. Raising my hand with trepidation, I asked Mrs. Evans what I should do when I simply could not understand! Her words immediately lifted my spirits. She told me that she remembered Mrs. John R. Rice telling someone whom she was trying to help, "I cannot possibly understand what you have been through, but I can care!"

"Wow!" I thought. "Now that is something I can do." I had already begun to love the girls on my dormitory floor, and I knew that I could care even when I did not understand.

To this day, I am faced with many people whose circumstances I simply do not understand. Working in the bus ministry and going soul winning puts me face to face with people from all aspects of society. There is no way that I could begin to understand all of the problems that are the reality for these dear ones for whom Jesus died. However, I can honestly say that I care enough to do what I can to reach the lost and to get them involved in church. I can also assure them that there is a God in Heaven Who always understands.

While there is no way you can fully understand the hurt someone is experiencing through a trial or grief, the most important thing is that you make them feel that you care.

1. Don't try to prove that you completely understand their situation. You probably don't.
2. Rather, reassure the hurting person of your love and your concern. Let them know you will keep them in your prayers and then do so.
3. Romans 1:9 says, *"For God is my witness, whom I serve with my spirit in the gospel of his Son, that without ceasing I make mention of you always in my prayers."* Prayer is one of the greatest resources we have for hurting people. At times it seems people almost apologize that all they can do is pray. Never apologize that all you can do is pray. When we pray for someone, we are calling on the great Creator God to solve the problem! It can't get any better than the fact that we can intercede on behalf of someone to the God of gods!

Rena Thomas Fish was first captivated by Marlene Evans' voice and her teaching when as a 12-year-old girl her pastor's wife purchased a set of "The Five Sins of Christian Women" and invited all the ladies and teenage girls of the church to listen to the tapes in the pastor's home. The following summer, Rena attended Youth Conference for the first time, and when Mrs. Evans briefly spoke to the teenagers, she sat on the edge of her seat to discover just what was so captivating about Mrs. Evans.

After graduating from Dr. and Mrs. Wendell Evans' alma mater, Tennessee Temple University, Rena transferred to Hyles-Anderson College to earn her master's degree in education. She was hired to work as a dormitory supervisor in 1985 and continued until her marriage in 1987. Mrs. Evans was the dean of women, and she was vitally involved with hands-on training when needs arose in the dorms.

The Importance of Being Friendly
by Gina Eyer

When I first enrolled in Hyles-Anderson College, I was so scared to talk to people. I did not know where the restroom was, and because I was afraid to talk to people, I wouldn't even ask anyone where it was! Every day on the way home, I had to stop at a gas station because I wasn't about to ask anyone at the college where the restroom was. I was too scared to look for one for fear I would get lost and have to ask for directions.

I took one of Marlene Evans' classes the very first semester I came to college. In that class she taught about how to be friendly to everyone. She didn't just tell us to be friendly; she showed us how to be friendly. She taught friendliness through the basic concept of taking one step at a time. She said that a shy person did not have to immediately go out in the halls and say, "Hi, how are you!" to everyone who passed. Rather, she taught to start by at least looking at everyone and smiling. She said, "If you can only look at one person and smile, then look at one person and smile. The next time look at two people and smile."

She also taught us many reasons why we should be friendly and why it is wrong not to be friendly. Then, she showed us by her example. When the class was concluded, she left the room and was friendly to everyone she met in the halls at the college. She may not have had time to talk to everyone, but she made time to greet everyone she met. She never made a person feel that she was rushed. Each semester I registered for at least one class she taught, and through her teaching she inspired me to be even a little more friendly. She believed in being friendly so much that she taught the principle in all of her classes.

I recently shared this story with someone who could not believe I had ever been that shy. After I had taken all of Mrs. Evans' classes for credit, I took them as audit classes so that I could keep learning from her. I learned something new in every class I had the privilege of attending. Mrs. Evans not only understood Proverbs 18:24, *"A man that hath friends must shew himself friendly...."*; but she applied Proverbs 18:24 to her life.

1. Being friendly is not a characteristic that is limited to those with outgoing personalities. It is important to realize that if you are a shy person, you do not have to completely change your personality to become a "friendly" person.
2. Take Mrs. Evans' advice and begin by taking baby steps.
3. Start by looking at people and smiling.
4. As you gain confidence, start saying "Hi" when you come in contact with people.
5. Continue to grow in the area of speaking to people and smiling. You probably will never be a big talker, but there is a great need for people who will look, smile, and then listen! There are no "waiting lines" in the area of being a listener.

Gina Eyer graduated from Hyles-Anderson College in 1996. She was hired to work as Mrs. Evans' secretary in 1998 and served in that capacity until Mrs. Evans' death in 2001. Gina now works as Christian Womanhood's customer service manager.

Are You Making a Difference?
by Gina Eyer

My grandmother sent my father an article which had been written about my grandfather on April 11, 2002, in *The Woodford Sun*, a Versailles, Kentucky, newspaper. For 32 years, my grandfather was a preacher in Midway, a small town in Kentucky with an approximate population of 800.

I was surprised to see the article because my grandfather died 21 years ago. His wife, sons, grandchildren, and great-grandchildren now live in Indiana. I found it amazing that 21 years after his death, someone would write about a preacher who had pastored a small church in a small town.

As I read the article to my mother, tears welled in her eyes. I was four years old when my grandfather died, but he had already made a big impression on my life—just as he did on the life of everyone with whom he came in contact. Like Marlene Evans and Dr. Jack Hyles, he loved people; he helped people. At his funeral, several people related to my father things that my grandpa had done for them. "Your dad paid for our electricity," one said. "Your dad bought us groceries," another said. On and on the stories were told.

People have told me over and over again how my grandfather was an extremely law-abiding citizen. When the whole family "jaywalked" across the middle of the street, my grandfather walked to the corner and crossed in the proper crosswalk. (By the way, jaywalking is against the law.)

In *The Woodford Sun*, my grandfather was quoted as saying, "As minister of this church, I've probably ministered to about 500 people during these years in Midway and probably performed about 240 weddings. I feel that I've been blessed by serving the Lord and would choose this mission again if I were starting out as a young person."

The week after I received the article was Mother's Day, and I went to visit my grandmother. My cousin Paul was preaching that night at their church. His sermon was about having compassion enough to give the Gospel to the lost. Paul was ten years old when our grandfather died. He remembers him much better than I do. As I listened to Paul preach, I thought, "He really caught what Grandpa was all about." I see our grandfather in Heaven elbowing Paul the Apostle and saying, "Hey! That's my grandson preaching the Gospel!"

It is not important whether or not you are a well-known speaker like Mrs. Evans. What is important is whether or not you make a difference in the lives of others like my grandfather and Mrs. Evans have. Twenty-one years from now, Dr. Hyles and Mrs. Evans will be remembered for some of the same reasons that an article in a secular newspaper was written about my grandfather. The following statements characterized Dr. Hyles, Mrs. Evans, and my grandfather:

1. **They obeyed authority no matter how inconvenient it was for them.** If Grandpa had to walk an extra mile in order to keep from jaywalking, he would have. Brother Hyles drove the speed limit because it was the law. Mrs. Evans changed what she was doing midstream with no questions asked because of a request by the authority. One of the best ways to obey God is to obey the higher authorities.

2. **They did not complain about the ministry.** My dad never heard his father complain about the ministry. I never heard Mrs. Evans complain. Dr. Hyles, Mrs. Evans, and my grandfather loved the ministry and people. They thought it was an honor to serve God and His people. The ministry is people. Of course, I am not referring only to full-time Christian workers. If you are a soul

winner, Sunday school teacher, nursery worker, or bus worker, you are in the ministry. People can tell whether or not you care.

3. They were not interested in praise. Dr. Hyles, Mrs. Evans, and my grandfather just wanted to help people. If an individual was a little different, they saw that person as someone designed by God. They loved people, and they were more interested in seeing people grow than seeing their works grow. Much of what they did for others will never be recorded on earth; however, someday in Heaven, we will know all that they did. We will all be amazed. Even though Brother Hyles had a large church, the members knew that he loved them as individuals.

I doubt that anyone reading this article has ever heard of Raymond Eyer, but he made a difference in Midway, Kentucky. If you are remembered 21 years from today, for what will you be remembered? The key is that Dr. Jack Hyles, Mrs. Marlene Evans, and Raymond Eyer were not trying to be remembered. They were just trying to serve God and others. Their whole life was about serving God. It surely is amazing that when you serve God, you have to serve other people, and when you serve others, you make a difference in their lives. Are you making an eternal difference in others' lives? Will anyone remember you 21 years from today?

She Tuned in to Others
by Dianne Smith Dowdey

My husband and I went to visit Aunt Marlene on the Friday night (1½ days) before she passed away. Something I said made her think we wanted to bring in Schoop's hamburgers. She said, "Yes! I believe I could do Schoop's." She was barely able to talk coherently because of her pain medications and because she was so weak. Still, she was not going to put a wet blanket on my fun plans.

My aunt was so unique in that she always responded positively to any ideas that were proposed. If she could possibly join in, she did. If the circumstances would not permit her to join in, she found a way to be supportive.

One evening my husband decided to take our family for a ride to downtown Chicago—just to see the sights. We invited Aunt Marlene, but she could not go with us. She insisted, however, that we take her car. "Open the moon roof so you can see the tall buildings through it!" she excitedly said. "Also, if you happen to stop at Garrett's (our favorite popcorn place), I'll take a small bag. Just leave it at my door."

It was not difficult to agree to her small request! As we were about to leave, she added another wish: "When you kids get back, I want a detailed report of all that happens so I can enjoy thinking about what you got to do."

Aunt Marlene loved to receive "reports." She made us feel like we were really doing something for her when all we did was have fun and share the happening with her. As she was receiving her report, nothing else mattered but what we had to say. She knew how to "tune in" to those who entered her life.

Building close relationships takes work. Close relationships do not just happen; they are developed on purpose. It seems that one of the most common of relationship problems is the mother-daughter relationship. It is not uncommon for daughters not to feel close to their mothers and vice versa.

1. Listening is one of the best ways to make someone feel you really care about them. It is a key to building close relationships. Listening happens on purpose.

2. The word *hear* is used 550 times in the Bible. (That total does not include variations such as "hearing" or "heard.") Four times in the Gospels Jesus said, *"He that hath ears to hear, let him hear."*

3. One cannot properly respond in a way that makes people feel loved if he is not really listening.

4. Learn the discipline of being a great listener. As much as Marlene Evans was known as a big personality who had lots of exciting things to say, all who knew her well knew that she was one of the best listeners they had ever met.

Marlene Evans enjoyed reading to her great-nephew, Chad Dowdey.

Dianne Smith Dowdey is the only daughter of Jerry and Doris Smith, who also have one son Mike. As a child, Dianne always wanted to be around her Aunt Marlene and be involved in whatever she was doing. As a young adult, Dianne began to see and understand how much effort it took and how unselfish her aunt was in her fun. Dianne's interest only grew greater as she realized that her aunt worked hard at the fun she had because she wanted to make other people's lives better, and fun was just one of her many tools.

Photo: Mrs. Evans joined several of her family members for a fall bicycling activity. (Left to right) Marlene Evans, granddaughter Amanda Evans, great-nephew Chad Dowdey, sister Doris Smith, and niece Dianne Dowdey.

Dianne Dowdey brought great-nephew Chad to visit his
Aunt Marlene and Uncle Wendell . (1996)

The three Zugmier sisters—Kathryn Emery, Doris Smith,
and Marlene Evans (l to r)

She Registered Approval
by Dianne Dowdey

My birthday party was at the end of June, just a few days before Aunt Marlene went to Heaven. She could not come to the party because she was too weak. At that time, she wasn't able to eat much because of the cancer tumors. She asked for a plate to be sent with a little bit of everything from the party. We knew her condition was sounding very bad; all of the signs told us she wouldn't be with us long. We knew she probably couldn't even eat the small portions she requested, but she wanted us to know she was supporting our fun.

I couldn't help but think of all the times we had experienced with her. Many times when we would invite her to a breakfast, we soon found she had already been to a couple of breakfast dates! She would come and order something to munch on or sip. She seemed so pleased to be able to be with us—even if it was her third breakfast! She never said, "I'm too full. Just go without me." She even pretended to eat something so we would be comfortable. If we teased her about so many breakfasts in one day, she responded, "I really like spending time in restaurants with people I love."

Sometimes we offered her something that we really liked from a restaurant. She would say, "Yes, I believe I'd like just a quarter of that," or "I'd love to have a taste of that." She was a great one for "halving" a dessert. Then her very expressive eyes registered approval of our choices.

My aunt knew the value of going along with as many suggestions as possible. She made us feel loved and accepted doing so. Her acceptance promoted a good time.

1. Support and encourage others' fun and creative thinking.
2. Never squelch or make light of any idea or suggestion.
3. Proverbs 3:27 states, *"Withhold not good from them to whom it is due, when it is in the power of thine hand to do it."* Encourage and support others every opportunity you have to do so.

Waiting in the Wings
by Leslie Beaman

Throughout my life, I have worked very hard to try to become a more balanced person. I believe I know where my strengths lie, and unfortunately, I have to say patience would not be on the top of my list! I remember an incident that happened during my second year on staff at Hyles-Anderson College. It seems like yesterday even though this event happened about 24 years ago. I was working with someone who always seemed to cut corners. Now mind you, I wasn't opposed to doing whatever it took to get the job done, but this guy even made me nervous! Not only did he always seem to bend the rules a bit, but he was known for coming in late, leaving early, and avoiding anything that he found unpleasant to do. It appeared at times that this guy was almost impossible to motivate. As a result, many others, myself included, had to pick up the jobs he was assigned to do.

After a while, I grew to really dislike the guy. Mrs. Evans sensed my displeasure and sat me down for a "chat" one day. She began, "Leslie, wherever you go, there will always be someone like so-and-so waiting in the wings."

I thought I understood what she meant, but I asked her to define "waiting in the wings."

She clarified by saying, "There will always be someone you think isn't carrying his weight. There will always be someone with whom you have difficulty getting along—someone you wish the boss would fire. Just remember, if it's not so-and-so, it will be someone else. There is always someone waiting in the wings."

I remember as if it were yesterday saying, "Thanks; that's a real comfort!"

She laughed and said, "I am trying to help you avoid being bitter or upset."

I then remember asking her, "So what's the answer? Bite my lip and shut up?!"

She shared some advice that was a real help, some advice that I have tried to remember whenever I'm tempted to get irritated with anyone. "Try to compare your weaknesses with the other person's strengths, instead of comparing your strengths to the other person's weakness."

I realize that I'm not everyone's cup of tea. I'm sure I have irritated my share of people with whom I have worked. (Please don't send in any testimonials!) If I wanted people to be patient with me, I needed to work on being patient with others.

It all made sense to me. There will never be a perfect situation when you are working in a world with imperfect people. How could there be? So, as soon as one problem leaves your life, there will always be another one waiting in the wings to take over.

If you don't learn to "toughen" up and take things in perspective, you most certainly will stay bitter and upset. Is it any surprise that one of Marlene Evans' books is titled *Relationships Without Regrets?* She had few regrets in the area of human relationships because she learned how to deal with many different kinds of people with great success.

Great relationships take hard work and prayer, and always keep in mind, there is never a perfect situation in this imperfect world of ours. Someone will always be waiting in the wings.

Working with people is always a challenge. Different personalities, backgrounds, mind-sets, levels of spiritual maturity, work ethics, and idiosyncrasies are all opportunities for frustration. Keeping the following principles in mind will help you be able to work more effectively with people:

1. One of the root causes of problems in working with people is pride. Proverbs 13:10 says, *"Only by pride cometh contention: but with the well advised is wisdom."* It is human nature for a person to feel he is right. Pride refuses to look at the other person's point of view, or to admit that he may be wrong, or for that matter, to be patient with someone who is wrong and is not doing what he is supposed to do.

2. Therefore, it takes true humility to work smoothly with people. Of course, Jesus is our model as explained in Philippians 2:8 which says, *"And being found in fashion as a man, he humbled himself, and became obedient unto death, even the death of the cross."* Jesus was the sinless, perfect Son of God, and He humbled Himself that we might have eternal life. Surely we who are sinners should humble ourselves in working with people.

3. We often get impatient with people who do not perform as we do. Sometimes we expect people to do what we ourselves have not done. They may be weak in an area where we are strong, but all of us have weak areas that need work. When feeling impatient with someone who doesn't do just as you think they should, remind yourself of an area where you struggle.

4. It would do us well to remember what God does when He considers people. Psalm 103:14 says, *"For he knoweth our frame; he remembereth that we are dust."*

Don't Take Up My Cause
by Leslie Beaman

I guess it would have to be said that I am, and in some small ways always will be, the "great crusader for lost causes." Before I became a Christian, I was a great one for campaigning for worthless endeavors of all kinds. I remember one of my stupider (if that's a word) moments was when I formed a "sit-in" at my public high school protesting for longer lunch times (I told you it was stupid!). After I had been a Christian for a grand total of six months, I started attending Hyles-Anderson College. My life was truly transformed while getting my education at the college and under the preaching of its chancellor and pastor, Dr. Jack Hyles.

I remember the first time I heard someone criticizing First Baptist Church, Hyles-Anderson College, and the godly teachers I had grown to love and for whom I felt so grateful. I wanted to pull that person's heart out of her chest and show it to her as it beat for its last time.

I remember one Christian Womanhood Ladies' Spectacular as if it were yesterday. I believe it was one of the very first or second Spectaculars conducted by Marlene Evans. I was standing two or three feet away from someone who didn't have a good word to say about Mrs. Evans or the Spectacular. I couldn't imagine in my wildest dreams that anyone would ever dislike the woman I owed so much to! This delegate was tearing apart someone who had made an unbelievable difference in my life.

To say the least, I became totally enraged! I let the lady know where the exit was and told her that she was free to leave at any time. It was one of my proudest moments...until Mrs. Evans heard about it.

I didn't expect a trophy or an engraved plaque or flowers, but I surely didn't expect Mrs. Evans' reaction. For at least 30 minutes, she chewed me up and spit me out. The following are a few of the choice words of wisdom that I remember Mrs. Evans imparting to me that day:

"Leslie, don't ever take up my cause like that again! I am not everyone's cup of tea. I do not have universal appeal, and from time to time, people are not going to be happy with me. Bite your lip and let it go. You hurt me more when you try to defend me."

Wow! What in the world was that all about? "Don't take up my cause." Why would she say that?! I mean for the first time in my life, I was crusading for something of value, and I get slammed for it?!

Now I'll have to admit some 30 years later, I still want to deck the person when he or she criticizes a godly leader I've grown to love, but I've realized through the years that Mrs. Evans was **so** right. We as Christians can't keep fighting and taking up people's causes. When would it stop?

I can't tell you how many times I've wanted to take up my husband's or my children's causes with different people. I can't tell you how many times I've thanked God that I didn't do it. Mrs. Evans would always tell me to choose my battles wisely.

There are times when you need to stand up and make your opinions known, but there are many more times when you need to bite your lip and go on. I don't know if any of us will ever be effective Christians as long as we are taking up causes and fighting over meaningless endeavors.

In the words of Marlene Evans, "Choose your battles wisely," and for the most part, "Bite your lip and go on!"

1. As Christians we cannot properly represent Christ if we are always fighting to make things right on our own.

Remember, God is in control!

2. When you are tempted to interfere where it is not your place, bite your lip and go on!
3. Don't try to fight other people's battles; God has given each us plenty of our own to fight!
4. Remember Romans 12:19b which says, "...*Vengeance is mine; I will repay, saith the Lord.*"

$\mathcal{A}$nger
by Leslie Beaman

$\mathcal{A}$NGER—I have the mug, the magnet, and the t-shirt…been there!

Lately I find myself missing Marlene Evans quite a bit. The Lord used her in so many ways in my life. She was definitely a wonderful teacher and a mentor to me. Yesterday I was in a hurry (nothing new). My younger son was in the car. I pulled out of the garage, started to back up, and then it happened. I felt a jerk forward.

"What was that?" I yelled.

To my heart-sickening realization, I had just backed my car into my older son's car. He had been instructed to park his car in front of our house and not in the driveway—on more than one occasion. I can't tell you how displeased I was at that very moment.

This was a wonderful opportunity for me to show my children how to handle life's frustrations, and I failed miserably because I was angry at myself, at my older son—at everything. How sad.

After my "mini-fit," I got back into the car and decided to take my younger son out to breakfast. (I was in a "cool-down" mode.) I was very quiet. After a few minutes, I started talking with my younger son. "Adam, I handled that situation with Drew's car very badly this morning. The Lord wouldn't have been pleased."

We discussed the situation a bit longer, ate breakfast, and went back to the house. I discussed the situation with my older son. We both had made errors in judgment. I can't tell you how disappointed I was in myself. Children learn so much from what we tell them, but they learn far more from what we show them. In other words, our actions are speaking so loudly, they can't hear a word we say. ANGER can destroy a relationship quicker than almost anything.

As I thought through this situation, I thought about Mrs. Evans and what she would have said. I can just hear her say, "Get things right and go on!" She also would have reminded me of a lot of verses that deal with anger.

What does it take to set you off? In the scheme of things, is it really worth all the stress and frustration? You'll lose far more than you'll ever know. A dent in a brand-new car can be repaired. The damage from angry words leave permanent scars.

1. When an unexpected negative event occurs, bite your tongue. There's always plenty of time to talk later, but you can never recall words once they have been spoken.

2. Think before you speak. Plan your response. When planning your response, realize that correction or "I told you so" is usually interpreted as rejection. Again, you can always correct later; choose words that will help repair the situation.

3. Think in solutions. Just repeating all the negative does nothing but reinforce that there is a problem—so as quickly as possible figure out ways to correct the problem.

4. Keep in mind that people are more important than things. Whatever or however big the problem, the people involved are the priority.

5. Ephesians 5:32 says, "*And be ye kind one to another, tender-hearted, forgiving one another, even as God for Christ's sake hath forgiven you.*

Life's Distractions
by Leslie Beaman

Cell phones, navigational systems, DVDs, CDs, palm pilots, I-pods, MP3 players, computers, e-mail, text messages, and on and on it goes. Wow! We have come a long way. Kids are no longer counting cows or reading books on long trips. Now they have electronic game units, DVDs and MP3 players. They don't even have to think. We have programs that will do it for them. It seems like everything kids could possibly have in the form of entertainment has been given to them. How scary!

Now I'd be lying if I said I don't love air conditioning on hot days, and yes, I'll admit I would like knowing that if my car ever broke down I could use my cell phone and call for help without ever having to leave the safety of my vehicle. And aren't navigation systems great—if you can learn how to work them? HA! Yes, a lot of these items I mentioned can be such a blessing. They also can be a huge distraction. They can take us away from family, friends, parents, kids, etc.

I remember one time Mrs. Evans drove to Toledo to see me. We walked into our favorite restaurant, sat down, ordered our food, and began talking. Then it happened! My cell phone rang. I answered it, and when I looked up, I saw it! It was **the glare**. Yes, the horrible, bone-shaking, stomach-turning, eye-watering glare coming from Mrs. Evans. If looks could kill, I was dead.

I quickly got off the phone and said, "WHAT?"

She informed me she hadn't driven hundreds of miles from home to stop by and watch someone talk on a cell phone. To say the least, I got the hint. I turned off the cell phone, and never again, and I mean NEVER again, did I have it on in her presence.

If you have a cell phone, and believe me they can be a wonderful tool, you have to have the power to set up rules for usage. If you're with your husband, shut the thing off.

Occasionally one of our sons will call us when my husband and I are out together at a restaurant. I always try to have my husband talk with him because then it's usually two questions and two answers, and they hang up. I once heard a widow say after selling her home she had owned for many years, "I sold my home because I found my home owned me; I didn't own it."

In other words, her life was being lived maintaining a home, and she found she could do very little outside of house upkeep. She was smart in selling her house as she found it "controlled" her and took more from her than she was willing to give. I am afraid one day we are all going to wake up and realize we've really lost out in life. We've missed all the important things in life because we let life's distractions control us.

Let me ask you a question. Does your cell phone, MP3 player, computer, etc. own you, or do you own it? Who's in control? Yes, it's rude—plain rude—to go out to lunch with someone and be on the cell phone talking with someone else. Mrs. Evans was so right. Don't let life's distractions take you away from your relationship with the Lord, your spouse, your family, or your friends. All these electronic gadgets I've mentioned can be a wonderful tool if they are used properly and in moderation.

My husband is in charge of our college-age singles class at Lewis Avenue Baptist Church. We discussed the fact that maybe at our next activity we should have a big basket at the door and tell everyone who attends to please place all cell phones and other electronic gadgets in the basket. They can pick them up when the activity is over. Ha! This way, instead of "texting" the young adults who didn't come to the activity, each attendee would be forced to talk to the ones who did come.

Remember, it's all about control. What controls you? Don't let life's distractions rob you of the wonders God has in store for you each and every day.

1. When you are with people, be sure you are really with them.
2. Practice good manners when you are with people. Resist the temptation to be "plugged into" your electronic equipment.
3. Realize that being plugged into your electronic equipment rather than the people you are with is a form of rejection. It makes the statement that they are not important to you.
4. If you do need to make or receive a phone call (which should be on rare occasions), step away from the person or people, make the call as brief as possible, and return to the people you were with as quickly as possible.

A Round Table Discussion
by Leslie Beaman

Marlene Evans loved restaurants. This may have been due to her background. Her father owned a restaurant, and as she was growing up, Mrs. Evans often sat in a booth and did her homework and also worked long hours as a waitress at that restaurant. Maybe she loved restaurants because she loved people and great conversations, and she used restaurants as a way to **create**, **plan**, and **discuss** ways to make everything around her run smoother, and everyone around her live happier and become more successful in God's service. Mrs. Evans had a list of top ten restaurants she liked which she updated from time to time. In the Toledo, Ohio-Temperance, Michigan, area where I live, the list went like this:

1. The Hathaway House in Blissfield, Michigan
2. J. Alexanders in Toledo, Ohio
3. Café Marie in Toledo, Ohio (for breakfast)

In Indiana the list was different. At times it might have been Strongbow Turkey Inn, Teibel's, or Cracker Barrel. One thing was for sure: if she was with a large group, Mrs. Evans always wanted a round table—at least she did every time I was with her. She liked round tables because everyone could see each other's faces. She felt it made for better conversation. She never wanted to exclude anyone; every person's opinion was important to her. To Mrs. Evans, the seemingly most insignificant person was just as important as the "Queen of England"—probably more so.

Mrs. Evans always went out of her way to focus on those to whom the majority of people wouldn't stop to speak. She always seemed to love the unlovely. Mrs. Evans was a spiritual carpenter.

She spent her life, with God's help, trying to repair broken people. Anyone who ever spent more than an hour with her knew that she put great value on all of God's creations—every living thing. I guess that it would only make sense that she would prefer to sit at a round table and avoid a "head table" or "preferred seating."

It was her way of saying, "Everyone at my table **matters**, and we are all on the same level in God's eyes."

Treating all people like they are important is a lofty goal and one we should all try to attain.

1. Remember that God is not a respecter of persons. Acts 10:34 says, *"Then Peter opened his mouth, and said, Of a truth I perceive that God is no respecter of persons."*

2. Since we are to be Christlike in our actions, we should not be a respecter of persons. James 2:1-4 says, *"My brethren, have not the faith of our Lord Jesus Christ, the Lord of glory, with respect of persons. For if there come unto your assembly a man with a gold ring, in goodly apparel, and there come in also a poor man in vile raiment; And ye have respect to him that weareth the gay clothing, and say unto him, Sit thou here in a good place; and say to the poor, Stand thou there, or sit here under my footstool: Are ye not then partial in yourselves, and are become judges of evil thoughts?"*

3. People who are respecters of persons are full of pride. Only pride could make one think that he is better than someone else. Psalm 103:14 tells us, *"For he knoweth our frame; he remembereth that we are dust."* The fact is, we are all just dust. If He, the Holy One of Israel, can remember that fact, certainly we should also!

4. Remember that we are all God's highest creation and each of us is made in His image.

5. If someone appears "unlovely" or seems to feel uncomfortable in a situation, go out of your way to make the person feel loved and cared for.
6. Pay close attention to the people around you; study what they need from you, and then do all you can to meet those needs.

Mrs. Evans joined her family members at the Lakeside Cafe in Cedar Lake, Indiana, to celebrate her sister Doris' birthday in August 1998. Notice the round table!
(Pictured left to right: Marlene Evans holding Chad Dowdey, Doris Smith, Chip Dowdey, and Dianne Smith Dowdey)

Her Silence Spoke Volumes— When Correcting
by Leslie Beaman

Anyone who knew Marlene Evans knew her silence said a lot more than most people's words. Unfortunately, my behavior as a college student seemed to bring out many long, silent moments from Mrs. Evans. If you were in her presence at one of these long, quiet moments, you found yourself wishing you were almost anywhere else—Iran, Iraq, North Korea, anywhere.

At one such moment, I was called into her office. She let me stand in front of her for what seemed like an eternity as she looked down at some papers, read through some notes, etc., until she looked up at me. By this time I was sweating, and though my memory has failed with time, I believe I was shaking. It's a huge deal being called into the Dean of Women's Office, and this visit was no exception.

When Mrs. Evans finally spoke, she simply said something like, "What do you have to say for your behavior?" I began spilling my guts, apologizing for the incident to which she was referring, and then I went on to apologize for everything else I could think of! I don't remember this for a fact, but I probably apologized for things I was thinking of doing! You see, I not only respected Mrs. Evans' position, I respected **her**, and it pained me that I had let her down.

After teaching now for more than 20 years, I believe one of the biggest mistakes parents make when correcting a child is talking the child to death. Mrs. Evans always chose her words wisely, spoke briefly, administered punishment, and then restored you to fellowship. In the case to which I have been referring, Mrs. Evans also happened to show mercy. She told me that she didn't want to hear of my doing any more childish dormitory pranks. She paused for one more long moment of silence. Did I understand?

You bettcha! Her silence spoke volumes!

Our mouths can get us into trouble! Strive to be Christlike when correcting those under your authority—whether it is your own children, young people in a classroom, workers on a job, or those serving in a ministry with you.

1. Remember the Biblical principle in Proverbs 19:27 which says, "*He that hath knowledge spareth his words: and a man of understanding is of an excellent spirit.*"

2. Our God is merciful and although He cannot take away the punishment and consequences of sin, He does offer His help to make those consequences easier for us to bear.

3. Remember, when it comes to using words, often less is more—especially when it comes to correction!

Did I Tell You I Am Going to Die Soon?

by Leslie Beaman

A few years before Marlene Evans passed away, I drove to Schererville, Indiana, to spend a few days with her. It was summer, the weather was warm, and Mrs. Evans was enjoying a break between cancer treatments.

During my visit Mrs. Evans, a friend, and I drove to Chicago to eat at Lou Mitchell's, a unique breakfast place. Everything was going great, and then "it" happened. My friend and I were having a lot of fun exchanging "sarcastic barbs." I believe I was winning hands down when Mrs. Evans grabbed my hand and whispered, "Leslie, did I tell you I am going to die soon?" I was speechless. Of course I knew Mrs. Evans was going to die soon.

A few minutes later our conversation continued. It was my turn to return a classic slam, and then "it" happened again. Mrs. Evans grabbed my hand, leaned over, and whispered, "Leslie, did I tell you I am going to die soon?"

At that moment, my friend excused herself from the table. I turned to Mrs. Evans and asked, "Mrs. Evans, what is going on? What are you trying to say?"

"I'm not going to live long, and I don't want to waste one moment listening to two people I love tearing each other apart."

I wanted to say we were just joking. I wanted to say, "Hey, why don't you tell her? It takes two, you know?" I wanted to say a lot of things, but I said nothing. I just shut up and bit my lip the rest of the day. Mrs. Evans knew sarcastic joking can quickly turn into hurtful words, and she did not want our talk to get that close to negativity.

I sometimes wonder what we will most remember when we come to the end of our lives—the good things we have said or the critical words we cannot take back. It seems like I am constantly working on this area of my life.

Shortly before her death Mrs. Evans gave me a Bible with this verse underlined: *"Whereas ye know not what shall be on the morrow. For what is your life? It is even a vapour, that appeareth for a little time, and then vanisheth way."* (James 4:14) Maybe if we all lived our lives as if we had only a few brief moments left, we would guard our tongues more carefully.

1. Guard the words of your mouth. Your words can discourage and hurt or encourage and help someone's spirit.

2. Realize the words you speak come from your heart. Matthew 12:34b says, *"...for out of the abundance of the heart the mouth speaketh."*

3. Therefore, let Philippians 4:8 guide your thinking and your speech. *"Finally, brethren, whatsoever things are true, whatsoever things are honest, whatsoever things are just, whatsoever things are pure, whatsoever things are lovely, whatsoever things are of good report; if there be any virtue, and if there be any praise, think on these things."*

Being Gracious
by Julie Busby

When I was expecting my first child, my aunt and my mother came to Indiana from Canada for a visit. My aunt was the very first person I led to the Lord after I was saved. Shortly after I enrolled in Hyles-Anderson College, she was diagnosed with breast cancer. I had sent my aunt several books written by Marlene Evans; consequently, one of her requests when she visited was to meet Mrs. Evans in person. Mrs. Evans' health was not very good at the time, and I really didn't think it would be a possibility for my aunt and her to meet. After all, Mrs. Evans didn't even know me personally, nor did she know my aunt.

Unbelievably and graciously, Mrs. Evans invited us to her home to visit with her. What a magical time! She spent at least an hour with us just chatting about anything and everything. My aunt later told me that one of the happiest moments after her cancer diagnosis was the privilege of meeting Marlene Evans!

In 2006 on October 20, my aunt and one of my best friends died of cancer. Even though I miss my aunt so very much, I imagine Mrs. Evans, my aunt, and Dr. Jack Hyles, along with many others, just having a grand old time in Heaven—laughing and enjoying their new bodies and sitting at the feet of Jesus.

1. One of the keys to Marlene Evans' greatness was allowing God to use her cancer to help and encourage others.
2. I Peter 4:9a, *"Use hospitality one to another…."* Mrs. Evans opened her home and encouraged a fellow cancer buddy.

3. Rather than focusing on your trials, focus on the needs of others and do what you can to meet those needs.
4. Whatever trials come your way, ask God to use those trials to be a help and an encouragement to others.

The summer of 1994, Julie Silvestrone Busby enrolled in Hyles-Anderson College. Having only been saved for six months, attending Hyles-Anderson College was quite a "culture shock" for the new Christian. Julie took many of Mrs. Evans' classes because Marlene Evans made Julie feel like God even had a purpose for someone like her.

Julie was inspired by Marlene Evans to live life to the fullest for God. Her realness, transparency, passion, and humor made a tremendous impact on Julie. Much of the time Mrs. Evans taught her classes she was battling chemotherapy. Even so, life was still a happening wherever Mrs. Evans was! Julie graduated from Hyles-Anderson College in 1997 and now works as the marketing director for **Christian Womanhood**, the magazine Mrs. Evans started.

(Pictured left to right: Marlene Evans; Ann DiBiasi, who passed away on October 20, 2004, at the age of 56 from breast cancer; Julie Busby)

Making Life Happen!

Section 3
Principles for Life

"I'm going to live until I die!"

– Marlene Evans

Finding the Best in Others
by Doris Smith

Pastor Jack Hyles was definitely Marlene's coach from the pulpit. She claimed that, and I saw it time after time. Brother Hyles would preach a truth that we needed to implement in our lives, and it seemed that Marlene immediately put it into practice. One such truth she called "seeing gold glittering." This truth has made a big difference in the way I think about people who may not fit into "my mold."

Marlene talked to a person until she found an interest or a talent that person had. Each time she saw that person, she asked about that area in which he or she seemed to excel. It would not be long before the person had the confidence to tell a victory in that area. One particular person had a very nice voice but had never used it for public praise to God. Marlene heard the person sing and encouraged him to the point that now he is using his talent in our church. A young lady seemingly had nothing about which she could be proud. In talking with her, Marlene found out she could sew. Every time the girl wore a garment she had made, Marlene made much of it, and the young lady glowed. A young man seemed very quiet and withdrawn, but Marlene saw a glimmer of a comedian in him. As she made him aware of the ability, he became more proficient. He was able to use that talent for the Lord.

Often when talking to a person, she said, "You seem to do ___ well. You are really good at that." Sometimes that statement would be the opening of a new avenue for the person. Many of the people with whom she chatted were those whom others shunned. In her visit, she uncovered a nugget that encouraged the person to keep going. I would love to think that I was able to see an ability in an individual which would encourage that person to serve the Lord to the greatest of his potential, as I watched Marlene do many times.

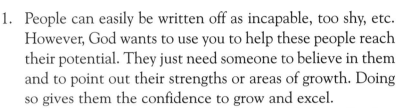

1. People can easily be written off as incapable, too shy, etc. However, God wants to use you to help these people reach their potential. They just need someone to believe in them and to point out their strengths or areas of growth. Doing so gives them the confidence to grow and excel.
2. Proverbs 20:5 says, *"Counsel in the heart of man is like deep water; but a man of understanding will draw it out."* There are people all around you who need to have someone "draw them out" so they can grow and reach their potential.

Marlene Evans and Doris Smith, enjoy life together!

Doris Smith called Marlene Evans "the ultimate big sister" who always looked out for the welfare of her baby sisters. Doris was an answer to Marlene's prayer for a little sister, so when Marlene enrolled in Bob Jones University and realized how much she was learning under the leadership of Dr. Bob Jones, Sr., she had to get Doris there. Doris had been planning to go to nursing school, so Marlene told her to come there for one year of nursing. Doris ended up staying and earning her teaching degree. The Evanses and the Smiths have worked together in the ministry of First Baptist Church of Hammond, Indiana, for 25 years.

Practicing How to Talk
by Carol Frye Tudor

One day I was driving from the college, and I glanced over to the car beside me to see Marlene Evans driving in the lane adjacent to me. I slowed down so I could drive next to her. I waved to her, trying to get her attention.

Mrs. Evans was obviously talking out loud, and she was gesturing with her hands as she talked. I looked to the passenger side of the car to see the person to whom she was talking. The seat was empty! I kept trying to get her attention, but Mrs. Evans was enthusiastically talking away while staring straight ahead and driving. The whole situation hit me as funny—I mean, I knew she loved to talk, and we loved to get together to talk. But this was the ultimate! She wanted to talk so much, she was enjoying talking to an empty car! She was obviously desperate!

Later I made a sarcastic remark about her talking, and she said, "Carol, I was practicing talking!"

"What do you mean practicing talking?"

"I want my words to count for eternity," she said. "I don't want to hurt people. I want to influence every person I'm around, so I have to practice what I am going to say."

Because of her influence on my life, I began a lifelong study of the book of Proverbs concerning the tongue. I took a red-colored pencil and marked every verse that includes any words having to do with talking such as "tongue," "lips," "words," "voice," and "mouth." I found there are over 100 verses on the tongue in the book of Proverbs. I found a verse that would fix every problem I have with my mouth if I would just use the solution!

Consider these five favorites of mine:

Proverbs 15:1, *"A soft answer turneth away wrath: but grievous words stir up anger."*

Proverbs 18:13, *"He that answereth a matter before he heareth it, it is folly and shame unto him."*

Proverbs 21:23, *"Whoso keepeth his mouth and his tongue keepeth his soul from troubles."*

Proverbs 27:14, *"He that blesseth his friend with a loud voice, rising early in the morning, it shall be counted a curse to him."*

Proverbs 29:20, *"Seest thou a man that is hasty in his words? there is more hope of a fool than of him."*

Yes, Mrs. Evans and her crazy ideas often tickled my funny bone, but as I used her methods, I found them to be practical and simple. I pray I can be the positive influence she was with her words.

1. One of the greatest ways we hurt others and limit our influence for eternity is by a poor choice of words. Proverbs 18:21says, *"Death and life are in the power of the tongue: and they that love it shall eat the fruit thereof."*

2. People who are known for their good words are people who plan their speech. Good words happen on purpose. Conversely, hurtful, damaging, "death" words are words carelessly spewed out without thought of consequences.

3. Think through what you are going to say to someone, especially if is a sensitive issue such as having to correct someone or address an issue that could be hurtful.

4. Remember, there is no merit in just saying everything that comes to mind. An out-of-control tongue destroys one's testimony and does great damage to the cause of Christ.

Lessons on Learning to Speak from Marlene Evans

by Frieda Cowling

Marlene Evans had a burden to help Christian women reach their potential and be all they could be for the Lord. Her influence upon my life was profound, and hardly a day goes by that I do not think of her and a lesson she tried to teach me.

Shortly after God moved our family to Indiana where my husband and I started teaching at Hyles-Anderson College, Mrs. Evans announced to me that she wanted me to speak to women. Even though I had taught for years, I realized I was not in her class as a speaker, so I told her I did not feel led to speak to women. Mrs. Evans said nothing else, and I thought the issue had ended. However, I underestimated her determination.

Not long after, Mrs. Evans invited me to go with her to a ladies' meeting in Flint, Michigan. I reminded her that I did not want to speak, and she said, "No problem." All the way to Michigan she interviewed me about my life, people we had reached for Christ, and how God had directed us to Indiana. I have never known a better listener than Mrs. Evans, and the time flew by.

We arrived at the church, and I found a seat near the front and settled down to enjoy hearing Mrs. Evans speak. Was I in for a surprise! The preliminaries were over, and Mrs. Evans walked to the podium. After a few opening remarks, she said, "Mrs. Cowling is going to come and share from her life how God used their family to reach people for Christ." I could not believe my ears and felt as if I were going to have a heart attack on the spot. I felt glued to my chair, but every lady in the church was staring at me, so I slowly walked to the podium. One look at my face and Mrs. Evans said, "I believe I will interview Mrs. Cowling instead of asking her to speak." She did, and somehow I lived through the ordeal. As we drove back to the motel that evening, I thought she might apologize for the trauma she had brought to my life. Nothing could be farther from the truth. As soon as we were in the car, she started helping me with my speaking with the following suggestions:

1. Hold the microphone close to your mouth like an ice cream cone so the ladies can hear you.
2. Speak up! You have something to say; and if you speak softly, no one will hear you.
3. Move your mouth when you speak and enunciate so people can understand you.
4. Be enthusiastic so people will want to hear what you have to say.

"One speaking experience is enough for me," I told her. She would not take "No" for an answer.

She replied, "God wants to use you to help women, and God wants me to help you."

I am not sure how much I have helped women, but I know she helped me. "I love you, Mrs. Evans."

When *Frieda Cowling joined the faculty of Hyles-Anderson College in 1977, she promptly went to Mrs. Evans' office to seek her advice because she wanted to be under her influence.*

Marlene Evans—the Life Changer
by Leslie Beaman

I once asked a fellow staff member at Hyles-Anderson College why she thought I was hired on staff. I don't know why I asked such a question; maybe it was because I wanted her to sing my praises. (Fat chance!) Maybe it was because I really wanted her opinion, or maybe it was because I could not imagine why I was hired in the first place. I certainly didn't fill the "staff bill." Whatever the reason (which now eludes me), I surely was not prepared for her response: "I think they hired you because they didn't want you running around saying you were a graduate." We both laughed, but I thought for years that maybe a bit of that was true!

I was saved just a few months before I hit the campus at Hyles-Anderson College, and I mean I hit the campus. I was only on campus for a few weeks, and I managed to flip a motorcycle and land in the hospital. It was at this time that I met Mrs. Marlene Evans, the dean of women.

I do not know to this day why she took me under her wing; maybe it was the fact that I was only two demerits away from being shipped home. Whatever the reason, she became my teacher, my mentor, and my dear friend. The "friend part" came much later! I won't go into my illustrious but tarnished college career. It's enough to say that when I made "Who's Who in American Colleges and Universities," they had to call my name several times before I realized they meant me.

When I was hired to be on staff, Mrs. Evans sat me down in her sweet, inimitable little way and said, "I want you to get a box and pack up all the clothes you have been wearing."

"What," I asked, "is wrong with my clothes? They are modest, and they've passed dress check. Besides, I am not the only one who dresses like this." Mrs. Evans patiently listened to all of my lame arguments as I desperately tried to convince her she was mistaken. When I was done speaking, Mrs. Evans began, "Leslie, I don't care who else wears clothes like the ones you have been wearing. I am not responsible for them; I am responsible for you. Yes, they may be modest, and they may have passed dress check, but when you wear them, you look like the 'world.' Faddish and worldly clothing make you look hard and rebellious. Is that really the impression you want to give as a new staff member or as a Christian for that matter?"

She did not give me a chance to answer that last question. She stood up and left. She just assumed that I would do what she said—and you know what? I did! I boxed up everything that I thought was questionable.

You may ask me what gave her the right to tell me what I should or should not wear. She had every right in the world. You see, I knew she loved me and wanted my best. I knew she knew a whole lot more than I did, and I respected her opinion more than almost anyone at that time. It never dawned on me not to do what she had asked.

I wanted to serve the Lord, and I wanted to be used of God. I wanted my life to matter, and if she thought a few skirts and tops were holding me back, they were gone! A few days after this appointment, I found a Norman Rockwell print of a little girl sitting in her slip, looking in a mirror. I bought the print, had it framed, and sent it to Mrs. Evans with a note that jokingly read, "All I have left is my slip. Is it okay if I keep it?"

I was told that when she received the picture, she laughed until she was almost sick. I am smiling as I write this just thinking of her reaction. This incident happened a little over 30 years ago, and it still seems like yesterday to me.

The week before I wrote this chapter, I received a package in the mail. When I opened it, I was surprised to find the Norman Rockwell print I had sent to Mrs. Evans many years ago. It seems that Dr. Evans thought I might want the print. I was given a bit of a surprise (as was Dr. Evans) when I read the following words written in Mrs. Evans' handwriting on the back of the picture: "When the time comes to give this away, please give it to Leslie Beaman."

I have cried buckets of tears looking at the picture and thinking, "Am I still the same girl who wants to serve the Lord and make a difference so much? Am I still willing to give up almost anything so God can use me? Am I still open enough to listen to others who want to help me?" And lastly and just as importantly, "Do I live my life so that others would take my word on something without question? Have I earned others' respect like Mrs. Evans had earned mine?"

This year marks my twenty-fifth year of teaching at State Line Christian School in Temperance, Michigan. There isn't a day that goes by that I do not stop and say, "Thank You, Lord, for Mrs. Evans. Please help me to remember the things she lived and the things she tried so hard to teach." I love her, and I miss her terribly.

1. No one really likes to take correction. It is humbling because it means you must admit you were wrong. However, correction from a leader is really a sign from God that He loves you. He wants you to reach your potential.

2. Psalm 141:5 says, *"Let the righteous smite me; it shall be a kindness: and let him reprove me; it shall be an excellent oil, which shall not break my head: for yet my prayer also shall be in their calamities."* It is a blessing from God to be correct-

ed by a leader. Correction will make us better people and more effective Christians if we accept the correction and make the instructed changes.

Who's Crowing in Your Life?

by Leslie Beaman

I have often said I'd rather learn from someone else's mistakes than learn from my own. I've heard time and again that there is wisdom in a multitude of counselors.

In Matthew 26:34 the Bible says, *"Jesus said unto him, Verily I say unto thee, That this night, before the cock crow, thou shalt deny me thrice."* As soon as the cock crowed, Peter knew he had done wrong. In this story the crowing of the cock was a shocking reminder to Peter that there is a payment we must pay for poor choices we make in life.

I don't believe anyone will ever grow if he just surrounds himself with people who always tell him whatever he wants to hear. Galatians 4:16 says, *"Am I therefore become your enemy, because I tell you the truth?"* I have been blessed to have people in my life who have crowed out long and hard whenever I planned on doing something they thought unwise or whenever I was heading down the wrong road. We all need someone who will crow out in our life like the cock did in Peter's life.

I teach high school students, and I laughed to myself when I overheard one high school boy announce, "I am sick of people telling me what to do. I can't wait to graduate, leave home, and join the Army." I never did ask him after he joined the Army if he was relieved that he no longer had anyone telling him what to do! HA! If you don't have anyone crowing in your life, if you don't have anyone who will stand up and tell you things you don't want to hear, **you are in trouble**.

Marlene Evans was that person in my life. She would crow long and hard if she thought I was about to make a foolish mistake. She would tell me when I was a young adult why she didn't think a certain guy was someone I should date. She would crow long and hard if I were hanging around the wrong crowd. She would crow long and hard because she knew I would listen to her. Mrs. Evans knew I would heed her advice—even when I didn't fully understand it.

I am much older now, but I still try to surround myself with people who aren't afraid to disagree with me. Now make sure when you pick people to "crow" in your life that they are:

1. People who love the Lord with all their heart.
2. People who really care about you and want you to succeed.
3. People who possess a great deal of godly wisdom.
4. People who are able to keep your conversations private. (Yes, they can keep their mouth shut.)
5. People who aren't afraid to speak up when they think you are doing something foolish or unwise.

So let me ask you—do you have anyone crowing in your life? Peter heard the cock crow **after** he had done wrong. Try listening to those who want to help you **before** you do something unwise.

Red Car Fever

by Leslie Beaman

If you have never been to our beautiful town of Toledo, you may have missed some of the great wonders of this world. We have a baseball team called "The Mud Hens," a hot dog place called "Tony's Packo's," a bunch of classic restaurants that sit right beside the muddy Maumee River (a sight to behold in the summertime), and a glass factory called "Libby." Yes, we have it all—the greatest zoo, fantastic Metro Parks, a world renowned art museum, and if you are ever bored, you can always go to "The Anderson Store" for the daily free samples! Yes, Toledo has it all except, of course, warmth. The winters are very hard. It's nothing to see someone wearing "coats"—yes, more than one at a time. I truly believe half of Florida is made up of Toledoians during the winter months.

All this to say, when the summer hits, we are ready! Off comes the black, and on with the lime green, bright orange, and hot pink! We are ready!

Marlene Evans used to say, "Leslie, watch out for 'red car fever.'" Every time summer has rolled around in Toledo for over 20 years, I've wanted to buy a red car...race around...run and scream, "The sun's back! The sun's back!"

I'm so glad Mrs. Evans always warned me, "Watch out for 'red car fever.'"

It seems like people do some of the stupidest things in the summer. They also wear things they'd never think of wearing in the winter. Not only are they void of coats; they are void of clothes altogether. Yes, in the summer more than any other time, people seem to be void of sense.

So if Mrs. Evans were here today, she'd warn you every time the summer rolls around, "Beware of 'red car fever.' " Remember that the same Lord you serve in the winter is the same Lord you should serve during the summer. Stay in church. Keep your standards, and avoid the "red car fever."

Every Christian is stuck with the old sin nature for all of their days on earth. It is important to realize that the sin nature automatically goes toward the path of least resistance. A person must live the victorious Christian life on purpose.

1. It is important to remember that God never changes. What was right in Genesis was right in the book of Revelation and is still right today. Malachi 3:6 says, *"For I am the LORD, I change not...."*

2. Therefore, we should learn what God expects in every area of our lives. That includes the way we talk, the places we go, the way we dress, and more.

3. Then we should put those principles into practice and, on purpose, continue to live those principles no matter what our circumstances, with whom we are spending time, or what season of the year it is.

We Just Don't Complain!
by Linda Stubblefield

The following story is an excerpt from Marlene Evans' book *The Five Sins of Christian Womanhood* about her Sunday school teacher at Highland Park Baptist Church, Mrs. Louise Holbrook, and the incredible impact she had on Mrs. Evans' life. Mrs. Evans faithfully passed on the principles she learned and gleaned from her teacher.

Mrs. Holbrook called me on the telephone daily and sometimes talked for an hour. In the course of our conversation, sooner or later I would start griping: "I don't like that Sunday school class!" "I don't like so-and-so." "I don't like what she does."

She would respond with, "Honey! Oh, honey!"

Mentally I would retort, "Oh honey, nothing! You don't see what those women do!"

Then she would add, "But we just don't gripe! We just don't complain! NO!"

Mrs. Louise Holbrook

And I'd say, "I do!"

As she drilled and drilled away and talked to me, she quoted: "*In every thing give thanks: for this is the will of God in Christ Jesus concerning you.*" (I Thessalonians 5:18) Finally, I'm glad to say, the teaching began to come through. Now it is my goal to live the kind of life that, no matter what happens to me, I rejoice in the Lord always. — Marlene Evans

My dream was realized—I was a January 1977 graduate of Hyles-Anderson College, and Mrs. Evans had hired me. Mostly I worked doing secretarial work in her "inner office" as she called it—a connecting nitch between her office and her secretary's office.

Mrs. Evans returned to the office from teaching a class, and Mrs. Linda Meister, her secretary at the time, said, "Mrs. Evans, you have a meeting this weekend."

"Are there materials packed? Are the papers stuffed?" (By "papers" she meant *Christian Womanhood,* a monthly publication for ladies.)

Mrs. Meister told Mrs. Evans that the packing was done, but the papers weren't ready.

"Linda Alexander," Mrs. Evans called, "come in here." When I walked into Mrs. Meister's office, she continued, "Would you please get 250 *Christian Womanhood* papers and stuff them with an order form and a subscription envelope?"

I sat down at a table and began to stuff the papers. I hated stuffing papers, though I was quick and I completed that kind of job quickly. As I stuffed, I started "commenting" under my breath. "I am a *graduate* of Hyles-Anderson College. I am above this kind of manual labor. I have a degree. She can get anyone to do this job...."

My back was to the connecting hallway between the offices, and Mrs. Evans had walked into her secretary's office—unbeknownst to me. Suddenly I felt a hand on my shoulder. When I glanced up and saw her, I was slightly mortified. "Linda," she quietly said, "if you would spend as much time praying that a life would be changed because of the impact of an issue of *Christian Womanhood* as you do griping, this world would stand a better chance of having some different women."

She turned and went back to her office. I quit griping and started praying. Mrs. Evans received her teaching from Mrs. Holbrook, "We just don't gripe! We just don't complain! No!" And she transferred this principle to me.

There are no "big" jobs and "little" jobs. Every job is a big job if it is for the Lord. Whatever your tasks, keep the following in mind:

1. Ecclesiastes 9:10a teaches us that every job we tackle is worthy of our best: "*Whatsoever thy hand findeth to do, do it with thy might….*"

2. Titles, degrees, promotions, and honors do not make us "above" certain tasks. It is pride that causes us to think we are at a stature in life where certain tasks are not worthy of our doing them.

3. An invaluable employee or volunteer is not the one who has the most degrees or qualifications for the job; it is the person who rolls her sleeves up and is willing to do whatever task is needed at the moment—whether it is changing diapers in the nursery, cleaning up the vomit of a sick child in Sunday school, or stuffing papers!

4. Usually the person who is chosen for a promotion or to fill a vacant position is the person who is willing to do whatever job needs to be done. Proverbs 29:23 says, "*A man's pride shall bring him low: but honour shall uphold the humble in spirit.*"

Making a Mark
by Leslie Beaman

All my life or ever since I can remember, I have wanted to make a difference. I remember as a child thinking if I wrote my name in different places, people would always remember who I was. Though I regret it now, I have carved my name on trees, wrote my name in wet cement, and even sprayed my name on the side of a bridge with the help of some friends. As far back as I can remember, I have always been aware that life is very short, and we only have a few brief moments to leave our mark. I guess I always wanted to believe that someday at my funeral, someone or several someones would remember who I was. Yes, I've always wanted my life to count for something. Unfortunately, I realize trees can be cut down, cement can be removed, bridges can be repainted, and names can be erased.

It wasn't until I met Marlene Evans that I learned what spiritual reproduction was all about. I learned that if I invested my life in someone else, I could make a difference for eternity with the Lord's help. Mrs. Evans wasn't big on bank accounts. She was big on investing all she had in the lives of others. She invested in others through her teaching, speaking, writing, and everyday living. Mrs. Evans carved her name on every life she invested in. I know because she carved her mark on my life as she did with hundreds of other students she taught.

You see, Mrs. Evans learned if you carve your name on people's lives, it would never be erased. I could use hundreds of examples of her investment in my life—as a student, as a young adult staff member at Hyles-Anderson College, as a newly married woman, as a mother of small children, etc.

One example that came to mind as I began writing this story was a time when I was just about to graduate from college. I was totally out of money and almost financially withdrawn from college. I was very close to losing all of my credits for the semester and being unable to graduate. Dr. and Mrs. Evans were never wealthy people, but they were always giving people. When I was told my school bill had been paid and I was now able to attend my classes once again, I knew immediately where the money had come from. I went to Mrs. Evans' office and waited for what seemed like hours. When she came out, I said, "Why? Why did you pay my school bill?"

"Dr. Evans and I believe in you," she said. "We wanted to have a small part in your future." I walked away determined not to waste their investment.

So long ago I stopped carving my name on trees, and with God's help, I have tried to make my mark where it counts most.

1. Jude 22 says, *"And of some have compassion, making a difference."*

2. By investing in people, you can make a difference for eternity.

3. The investments don't always have to be big productions or require huge amounts of time. You can make a difference by smiling at your child and saying, "I love you and I'm proud of you." You can make a difference by visiting a shut-in with a small gift. You can make a difference by befriending someone others make fun of. There are thousands of ways to make a difference—find them and make a difference.

Marlene Evans, My Boss
by Linda Meister

Marlene Evans and I started working together during the second year of Hyles-Anderson College. At the time the college was located in Schererville, Indiana, in the buildings that now house Hammond Baptist Grade School. Somehow she found out that I drove with our four children from Chicago every day to put them in Hammond Baptist Schools. She asked my husband if I would be willing to help her on a volunteer basis. Mrs. Evans helped me work out several complications so that I could work for her.

This was the beginning of my being Marlene Evans' secretary. I would carry her brown paper bag (she preferred brown paper grocery bags over a briefcase!) from classroom to classroom, take attendance, grade papers, or whatever she needed.

I knew Mrs. Evans when she had more energy than in her later years. She would come into the office after teaching a class, stand by my desk, and give me my orders for the next hour. If she didn't finish what she wanted to tell me, she would leave for class, walk very briskly down the hall continuing the list of projects while greeting the students, and I was frantically trying to write down what she was saying while dodging the students who were walking slowly. To work for Mrs. Evans meant that you had to have a pen and paper with you at all times. "Every good secretary always carries a pen and paper," she would say. I even learned to go to a wedding with pen and paper!

The entire Christian Womanhood staff took two different trips with Marlene Evans. On one of the trips, I drove and pulled a small U-Haul from Indiana to Dallas, Texas. The funny part was, I had never learned how to back up a trailer. I had to be sure I did not get into a situation where I would need to back up! I'm sure you can imagine a group of women packed in one vehicle pulling a U-Haul trailer.

The other trip the staff took together was to a meeting in Massachusetts. That time Mrs. Evans asked a pilot who was a member of our church to fly us there. What a trip! There were six of us in the plane. To change seats, one of us would have to sit on another person's lap. I don't think we laughed as much before or after that trip.

I've always been time conscious because I had been taught not to be late as a young child. Mrs. Evans held weekly meetings with her staff. During those meetings, I would keep my eye on my watch—that is, until Mrs. Evans noticed me watching the time. One day when I looked at my watch out of habit, she said, "Linda, please don't look at your watch again." Obviously, this habit of mine was distracting to her. It was one I immediately set to work on fixing.

Mrs. Evans taught me so much in the years I worked for her. I'll never forget the time I walked into a classroom, started to step up on the small platform, tripped, and fell. I was so embarrassed that I turned around and walked out of the classroom. Later that day she simply said, "Linda, you can never be a help to me if I always have to spend time putting you back together."

To this day, I still hear those words, and the memory helps me get beyond myself, my problems, and my embarrassment to be able to think of others.

1. Always have a pen and paper ready to write down ideas, thoughts, or reminders that come to mind. Mrs. Evans always feared that unless she wrote things down as she thought of them, she would forget them and never be able to recall the idea or thought.
2. Realize that sometimes idiosyncrasies (or good character traits such as being on time) can cause us to be distracting to a leader. Try to keep your eyes focused on the leader to help him keep his train of thought and to be a support to him.
3. Psalm 119:165 says, *"Great peace have they which love thy law: and nothing shall offend them."* People who "wear their feelings on their sleeves" cannot be used the way they could be if they refused to get offended or let an embarrassment keep them from doing the job they were assigned. It is not the leader's job to keep a follower's spirit "up." The follower is responsible for her spirit and her actions.

Linda Meister faithfully served as Marlene Evans' personal secretary until 1982, when her husband, Melvin Meister, accepted the pastorate of St. Amant Baptist Church, St. Amant, Louisiana.

Rubies—A Reminder

by Frieda Cowling

Marlene Evans loved rubies because she believed they represented the potential in every life that God wanted to develop. (She was God's right hand helper in this area in my life because I asked her to be.) Proverbs 31:10: *"Who can find a virtuous woman? for her price is far above rubies."* Proverbs 8:11: *"For wisdom is better than rubies; and all the things that may be desired are not to be compared to it."*

In 1977 when our family moved from Tennessee to Indiana, I went to Mrs. Evans and asked her to help me be more effective in serving God. She accepted the challenge, and at times I regretted having asked her (even though I knew she was right and was trying to help me.)

I had never had a goal of being a ladies' speaker, but Mrs. Evans and the Lord had another opinion. She called me and told me she wanted me to go with her to a ladies' meeting.

"I have no idea what to say," I told her.

"Don't worry about it because I'll help you know what to say," Mrs. Evans replied.

All the way to the meeting, she asked questions and listened as I answered them. As I think back on this, I'm sure she was worn out listening to someone talk for five hours straight, but she did not show it. "That's good—tell that," she would say. She divided my rambling thoughts into topics and was confident I could speak to the ladies (a confidence I did not share.)

I spoke, and she praised my feeble effort. She also admonished me to speak directly into the microphone, move my lips as I spoke, and speak louder. (If she said this once, I'm sure she said it a hundred times.) In fact, to this day, these instructions ring in my ears when I stand to teach a class or speak to anyone.

I still do not have a great desire to travel around and speak, but the opportunities I am given are because Mrs. Evans was convinced I had something to say to ladies (her words—not mine); and she was determined to help me learn to say that something effectively. I love you, Mrs. Evans. I never stand to speak without the desire to please you (and the Lord).

God has a plan for each of our lives. He leaves us on this earth after we are saved so that we can influence others for eternity. He wants to use us to make a difference in the lives of others. He wants us to win souls to Christ and influence Christians to reach their potential. Therefore, we ought to spend our days trying to fulfill God's plan for our lives.

1. Whom are you helping to reach his or her potential? If you are not investing in the lives of others, you are not fulfilling God's purpose for your being here.

2. Dr. Tom Vogel, the academic vice president of Hyles-Anderson College, often says, "The person doing the work is the person doing the learning." When you have a job to do, include those around you to help get the job done. That will help them reach their potential as they learn to do a task.

3. One of the greatest ways to build a people's self-esteem is to invest in them and help them reach their potential. Learning new abilities gives a people confidence and helps them want to learn more. View every task you have as an opportunity to help someone else reach his potential.

4. Oftentimes people don't want to ask others to help them on projects. Whether it is a matter of pride (where you want to do it yourself) or you feel others will feel you are

taking advantage of them, the fact is, you are preventing others from being used and from reaching their potential.

5. Some people may feel you are taking advantage of them, but your attitude will make a big difference. Being excited about the project, making the work together fun, and helping them learn new things will build them and make them happy to be a part of your projects.

After All These Years, I Can Still Hear Her Voice

by Leslie Beaman

It's Sunday night, church is over, and I have a few minutes. I have found myself missing you all day long. You see, Mrs. Evans, you know how I worry about stupid things that never even take place. Well, here I am again! Andrew is 18 now, and he is almost ready to head for college. I can almost hear your voice telling me not to borrow from tomorrow. I know what you are thinking, and I know you are right. Andrew will be fine! He will do his laundry and make his bed. And yes, I know he will do okay with his grades. I know you don't want me to worry about some stinking girl who may break his heart, but I do!

Did I tell you that Rick and I are building a house about a mile from the church? Yes, I can hear you. I wish I could tell you I am doing better with changes and that living in an apartment for the last five months hasn't even bothered me a bit! (Ha!) Who am I kidding? I know you are laughing; I can almost hear you at this very moment!

I am doing better. Remember what you always said? "Baby steps, Leslie. Just take baby steps."

Okay! Yes, I am doing that thing with my hair I do when I get nervous. I am glad you are not able to see it because it's not a pretty sight. Besides, no one ever even noticed I do it—except you. Nothing passes by you. You notice every little detail. I am trying to let things go that I cannot fix, and I am not a major perfectionist anymore. Well, maybe I still am, but I am working on that one.

I surely wish I could talk with you tonight. You've lived in the eye of the storm (with cancer) and managed to have such peace. I know you keep telling me over and over that God will give me what I need as I need it, as long as I trust in Him. I hear you, and I know you are right.

Dear Reader,
I am not losing my mind. I know Mrs. Evans went to Heaven in 2001. I hope you won't reserve a room for me in some psych ward when I tell you Mrs. Evans is still a part of my life. For years she was a mentor to me. She was such a godly teacher and friend, and at times like tonight, I really miss her presence, and yes, I can almost hear her voice.

1. One of Marlene Evans' greatest comforts through her cancer was that she would never have to really die. She took comfort in the truth of Hebrews 11:4b when God said of Abel, *"...and by it he being dead yet speaketh."*
2. When we invest in the lives of others, we can continue to influence even after we go to Heaven. Isaiah 30:21 states, *"And thine ears shall hear a word behind thee, saying, This is the way, walk ye in it, when ye turn to the right hand, and when ye turn to the left."*
3. Invest your life into the lives of others so that after your life on this earth is done you will still be influencing for eternity through the lives of those in whom you invested.

Speed Bumps
by Leslie Beaman

"Girls, if you live long enough, you will go through hard times."

I remember Marlene Evans making the above statement in ladies' split chapel in Hyles-Anderson College when I was just a teenager. I'd love to think I really listened way back then, but unfortunately, I think a lot of things just passed me by without much thought until years later.

I don't know if anyone can be fully prepared for the death of a parent, spouse, or child. How do you get ready for cancer, leukemia, or debilitating illnesses?

Some may ask how someone could prepare himself for a September 11 or for a hurricane that destroys his home, his church, or his entire town.

Mrs. Evans told me that I needed to get used to change because changes in life are inevitable. She went on to say that the only way you can prepare for life's tragedies is by making sure you're in the center of God's will doing what the Lord wants you to do daily.

I guess life is like driving on a road full of speed bumps. If you don't make adjustments for the speed bumps by slowing down, you will most certainly damage your vehicle. If you don't prepare yourself for life's heartaches by relying on the Lord and letting Him guide you, you will definitely destroy your life.

Tragedy and heartache come to us all. As Mrs. Evans once told me, "It's inevitable." How we handle those hard times will show the world on Whom we are relying.

"Speed Bumps" come to everyone. Plan and prepare for the challenges that lie ahead in your life and don't be surprised when they do come.

1. Changes come into everyone's life. Staying focused on Jesus Christ will help us be stable through these times. Hebrews 13:8 says, *"Jesus Christ the same yesterday, and to day, and for ever."*

2. Staying in the center of God's will makes changes easier to face.

3. How we handle the changes will show the world on whom we are depending. It will also be a testimony that we have something (i.e. Someone!) they need.

Veto Power
by Leslie Beaman

I heard someone say that it seems like most people make the biggest lifetime decisions at a time when they have the least amount of maturity. I am not sure if that's always true, but it does seem like people do a lot of foolish things when they are young. My pastor, Dr. Les Hobbins, has said at different occasions when talking to teens, "Go ahead and live it up; someday you will be trying to live it down."

I realized when at first attending Hyles-Anderson College, I could get into some major trouble if I didn't watch out. When I first began dating, I thought to myself, "I really don't know these guys at all." I didn't know their parents, their preachers, where they lived, or much about their background. My parents and preacher back home couldn't really give me much insight as they didn't know the guys either. I was advised on what warning signs to look for, but I must admit "attraction" can really gloss over troubled areas.

I decided to give Mrs. Evans veto power in my life. I really trusted her judgment and her opinion. She knew me, my strengths and my weaknesses, and she also had access to really check out some of the guys I would be dating. I wanted her to wave a red flag if she thought I was about to do something unwise.

I dated one guy who always seemed to have trouble paying his bills on time. His car, his school bill—you name it. This same guy dressed like a store catalog cover. The nicest shirts, ties, suits—WOW!—was he impressive and fun too. Mrs. Evans' only comment was, "If you marry him, your kids won't have shoes." I understood what she meant.

The next guy I dated had so much character. He worked hard, paid his bills, did everything right. You could depend on this guy. He was also very kind and thoughtful. Mrs. Evans said, "Leslie, so-and-so is a wonderful guy, but do you really see yourself with him?" I had dated him for over a year, and despite the fact that he was such a terrific person, I wasn't attracted to him as a possible life's mate. I was trying too hard to make it work, and she could see it.

I continued to date a lot of different guys, and some became very dear friends. One of the hardest relationships I went through was with someone for whom I began caring very deeply. I didn't ask anyone for an opinion—not even Mrs. Evans. I didn't want anyone's opinion. Mrs. Evans finally called me in for an appointment and said something I didn't really want to hear. "Leslie, I know so-and-so's parents pretty well. Honey, I don't understand it and never will, but I don't think they will ever accept you. Could you marry a person knowing his parents aren't 100% for you?"

The issues his parents opposed were areas I could not change—like the fact that I didn't become a Christian until I was 17 years old or the fact that some members of my family had problems with alcohol. It didn't seem to matter to them that I was a college staff member at the time. I hated the fact that Mrs. Evans was right! I didn't want anyone to be forced to choose between his parents and me. I knew enough to know that this relationship wasn't going to work.

We didn't say much more to each other as I left her office that day. I knew it was over; I knew she was right. I had chosen to give Mrs. Evans veto power in my life for a reason—she loved the Lord, and she possessed unbelievable insight into people. I met the man I would marry a year later.

This year marks our twenty-fifth anniversary. I love this man I married 25 years ago more each passing day. We are "Team BEA-

MAN." We have two wonderful children (young men now), and I cry when I think how blessed I am today.

If you are reading this article and you are between the ages of 12 and older, and you want to live a productive and happy life:

1. Live for the Lord.
2. Give someone whom you trust and respect in your life veto power over all the major decisions you make.

If you follow these two steps, I promise you will never be sorry, and you will have a lot less to regret later on in life.

There are times in life when we all have difficult decisions to make; following the principles listed below will help you make wise and godly choices:

1. Remember there are people who are older, have more experience, and have been where you are. These people should be the people you are looking to for advice.
2. Avoid the advice and counsel of your peers.
3. Let Proverbs 11:14 be your guideline in making decisions, *"Where no counsel is, the people fall: but in the multitude of counsellors there is safety."*

Stay Away From Fish Sticks and Green Jello

by Leslie Beaman

I worked in a nursing home with many elderly patients the summers of my freshman and sophomore years of college. I loved working with the patients, but I hated the conditions of the nursing home in which I worked. The building usually always had a terrible odor, and the rooms never seemed to be clean. What's more, the patients always appeared very unkempt.

I was always trying to change things. My supervisor's favorite line to me was "Leslie, don't rock the boat." I didn't want to rock the boat; I wanted to flip the boat over. I can't tell you much that I didn't want to change. For starters, the food was horrible. It seemed like every week without fail, they served fish sticks and green jello. (Yuck!)

I remember sneaking in dinner (Chinese food, cheeseburgers, etc.) to different patients. I often got in trouble for playing music in the dining hall—even though the patients loved it. I guess as bad as everything seemed, the one thing that made my heart sick was how some of the staff talked to the patients. They talked to them as if they were three year olds.

I realize some of the patients were hard of hearing and some were very forgetful at times, but I believe all of them deserved to be treated with respect and kindness. I am not saying all of the patients were easy to deal with. At times the work was very hard, and "thank yous" didn't come very often, but overall, I really liked working with the elderly patients.

My pastor and his wife, Dr. and Mrs. Les Hobbins, are in their seventies, and they still go on our high school senior trips—whitewater rafting, fourwheeling, etc. They love young people. Recently, several other teachers and I took a trip to the Museum of Science and Industry in Chicago with our high school juniors and seniors.

On the way home we stopped by the First Baptist Church of Hammond. Pastor Schaap invited all of the high school kids into his office. He served them snacks and drinks and let them sit behind his desk, pile on his couch, laugh, and have a great time. I was concerned because I felt our teens were really making a mess of Brother Schaap's office.

Brother Eddie Lapina, who was also there at the time, said, "This is nothing; you should see his office after our teens get done on Saturday mornings."

They don't do it on purpose, but teens can be messy. Mrs. Evans, like Brother Schaap, was more concerned with influencing people and less concerned about candy wrappers on the carpeting.

To Mrs. Evans, age was a state of mind. As far as I am concerned, she died a very young woman. She was ageless—a classic.

Now, I have to admit, I still shudder whenever I see a plate of fish sticks or get a glimpse of a bowl of green Jello. But I take great joy in knowing I can grow older, but I don't have to be old!

I remember talking with Mrs. Marlene Evans once about getting old. I told her how fearful I was of aging. I told her about the nursing home, and she said, "Leslie, you can grow older, but you don't have to be old."

"What do you mean?" I asked.

She shared the following thoughts with me.

1. **Don't talk old.** Mrs. Evans hated lines like "People our age shouldn't do such and such" or "You know we are all get-

ting older" or "Let's leave that for the youngsters." She hated when people would refer to someone as an "old man" or "old lady."

2. **Don't talk about all your aches and pains.** For example, don't say, "My back hurts" or "My legs ache" or "I am having bladder problems." On and on it goes.

3. **Never discuss your limitations.** I mean statements like, "I can't see like I used to." or "I can hardly walk anymore." A few years before Mrs. Evans passed away, she was riding on the back of a motorcycle, laughing like a teenager. I know she was limited physically, but that fact never seemed to stop her.

4. **Don't dress old.** Mrs. Evans always tried to be stylish and up-to-date. I don't mean she wore faddish clothes, but I do mean she tried to look her best at all times.

5. **Try to stay around kids and teenagers.** Mrs. Evans was not afraid of teenagers. She adored them, and they adored her. She took teens out to eat, went to the mall, sat down near them, and listened to them as they talked about whatever was on their hearts.

Are You Sick or What?

by Leslie Beaman

I once read a poem by Sara Teasdale that went like this:

> "They came to tell your faults to me,
> They named them over one by one;
> I laughed aloud when they were done,
> I knew them all so well before,—
> Oh, they were blind, too blind to see
> Your faults had made me love you more."

I used to wish I could remove some things in my life I considered faults. I started trying to become more like people I admired. Mrs. Evans one day inquired as to why I had become so quiet of late. I told her I felt I was too outgoing at times, and I wanted to be more like a person she and I both knew. Mrs. Evans with all her wisdom said, "Don't be stupid!" This was not the response I was expecting, and I must have shown it on my face.

If you were around Marlene Evans for very long, you knew when she was revving up for one of her "long talks." In this case, I'll give you the condensed version. "Leslie, all week long you've walked around quiet and almost mopey everywhere you've gone. Some people have thought you were sick; some have thought you were depressed. Are you telling me you've been doing this because you wanted to be more like so and so?"

By this time I was feeling pretty foolish, but I still managed to nod my head "yes."

Mrs. Evans added, "I am not saying there aren't things I think you should work on." She was always correcting what she referred to as my smart mouth. Unfortunately, I had a bad habit of saying the first thing that came to my mind, and that wasn't always a good thing.

She continued talking about how every one of us needs to continue with the Lord's help to work on areas in our lives that aren't pleasing to God. With that said, Mrs. Evans spent the rest of the time letting me know that even things we consider to be weaknesses can be used in a great way with the Lord's help.

Mrs. Evans was always someone to stress the balanced Christian life, becoming more well-rounded. I remember this talk Mrs. Evans and I had as if it were yesterday. I also remember as we were parting that she did say with a laugh, "If you want to have one of those 'quiet days' a few times each year, that would be okay with me." Then she laughed harder than usual. I didn't have to wonder what she was thinking.

When dealing with what you see as "faults" in your life, remember the following:

1. God made each of us unique and special. The things that set each of us apart from other people are not faults; they are God-given qualities to be used for His service.

2. Therefore, it is unwise to compare yourself with other people. II Corinthians 10:12 says, "*For we dare not make ourselves of the number, or compare ourselves with some that commend themselves: but they measuring themselves by themselves, and comparing themselves among themselves, are not wise.*"

3. Even my weaknesses can be used in a great way with God's help. II Corinthians 12:9 states, "*And he said unto me, My grace is sufficient for thee: for my strength is made perfect in weakness. Most gladly therefore will I rather glory in my infirmities, that the power of Christ may rest upon me.*"

4. Though we can learn from and emulate godly people, God

does not want us to be just like someone else. Rather, He wants us to become balanced, well-rounded Christians, letting Jesus be our example in Luke 2:52 which says, *"And Jesus increased in wisdom and stature, and in favour with God and man."*

I Want You to Be at Peace
by Leslie Beaman

Shortly before Marlene Evans went to be with the Lord, I sat by her fireplace. She was in her favorite chair, and we had a very long talk. I asked her a very difficult question. "Mrs. Evans, what do you think is lacking in my life in order for me to become a complete person?"

She didn't hesitate a bit. Mrs. Evans simply stated, "Leslie, I wish you could be at peace."

I cannot tell you what a jolt her words were. I guess she noticed my stunned disbelief, so she continued. She clarified by saying how happy she was that I had made things right with certain people in my family over the years. Alcoholism had taken its toll on my family and caused a lot of pain for everyone involved. She explained that she wished I could always have a peaceful spirit and a calmness in my life.

As a child I never could sit still much. I ate fast, played fast, and when I grew up, unfortunately at times, I drove fast. I was always running from one event to another.

While at Hyles-Anderson College, I worked in the area of student activities, and the job seemed to fit me to a tee. I planned events and programs and barely cleaned up from one when I'd have another. I realized Mrs. Evans' prayer for me was twofold. First of all, she wanted me to:

1. Slow down long enough to enjoy a sunset. She wanted me to stop running from one event to another and take in some of the everyday of my life with nature, my children, my husband, etc.

2. Stop trying to fix all of life's problems. She wanted me to rely on the Lord, hand my burdens over to Him, and let them go.

She wanted me to live calmly in the eye of the storm. She wanted me to live a peaceful life knowing there are some things I cannot change. I just need to go on living, recognizing the Lord is ultimately the One in charge.

Mrs. Evans was the perfect example of living peacefully no matter what the circumstances she found herself in. She knew she did not have long to live. She knew the cancer was taking its toll on her body, and yet she was able to hand her burdens to the Lord and show the world an inner peace few people have ever known.

Living with the Lord's peace isn't having your head in the clouds and being clueless to everything around you. Living with peace in your heart is being aware of the problems and burdens all around you, yet giving those burdens to God in exchange for His peace.

I have often asked myself how we, as Christians, ever hope to have much of an impact on a lost and dying world when we react to heartbreak the same way the world does.

My goal and prayer is to show the world an inner peace that only the Lord can give a person. "Yes, Mrs. Evans, I am still listening. I still hear you!"

1. Oftentimes people live their lives at a frenetic pace because they are trying to escape. They are trying to suppress the hurtful memories of a painful childhood, ignore problem relationships in their family, etc. However, this frenetic pace keeps peace at bay in one's life.

2. Slow down and enjoy the world God created for you. Take time to look at a sunrise, a sunset, a starry lit sky at night, the billowing clouds before a storm, the flowers of each season, birds, squirrels, etc.

3. I Timothy 6:17 states, *"Charge them that are rich in this world, that they be not highminded, nor trust in uncertain*

riches, but in the living God, who giveth us richly all things to enjoy." God has given us His creation for our pleasure and our enjoyment.

4. John 14:27 teaches that peace comes only from God. *"Peace I leave with you, my peace I give unto you: not as the world giveth, give I unto you. Let not your heart be troubled, neither let it be afraid."*

5. Getting to know God, His Word, and His Creation will help develop a relationship with Him. It will help bring healing to your wounded soul, and it will help bring lasting peace. It is His will for you to be at peace.

Section 4
Making Life Happen!

"If there is someone somewhere having a lot of fun, there is someone somewhere doing a lot of work."

– Marlene Evans

She Hugged Life Into Me

by Sheri Edwards

Every time I see Marlene Evans' face in the *Christian Womanhood* magazine, my heart just does a number. I was here in Brazil when she went to Heaven, and I am not sure if it really ever will hit me that she is not in Indiana still teaching and smiling. But my reason for writing is this:

When I was 16, I visited the campus of Hyles-Anderson College for the first time. As I walked through the front doors, a lady dressed in a flowing purple outfit and smelling of Beautiful perfume enveloped me in an embrace for no apparent reason other than she must have known that I was a visitor. I remember that moment as clearly as if it were yesterday—now almost 16 years ago. She welcomed me not knowing who I was, my name, or my background. She just hugged life "into" me, not out of me. Through the following years, this lady—Marlene Evans—became the woman I admired the most, counseled with the most, and looked at the most.

My last year of college, I was married and expecting my second child. Her cancer had returned, and we all listened to her tell us what was happening. She was weak (but would still have three more years to live). I remember sitting in the front row as she spoke. All of us ladies were trying to be brave, I suppose. I raised my hand and asked, "Are you saying we will have to watch you starve to death as you die?"

She just looked at me and said, "Yes." She didn't break down, step down, or look down. She just raised her eyebrows and answered our questions like it was the most normal happening. I stood with her that day and had someone take my picture. She was leaning into me, smiling, and her eyes were closed. She was hugging life back "into" me again.

My question is this: Who is hugging the girls now? Is there someone greeting the girls who don't even know who Marlene Evans was? Is someone remembering to hug life into a bunch of precious girls wandering the halls of Hyles-Anderson College? Mrs. Evans was a tremendous influence on my life.

I stood with an Indian woman who traded feather necklaces with me for used clothing. I also stood by an elderly lady as she picked out some used eyeglasses I brought back with me. I gave food to a baby. I bought clothes for a teenager and food for an older man working on our farm. But, I forgot to hug life into them...I forgot. I got busy and forgot.

1. In I Kings 20 the story of a servant who failed in his duties for the king is recorded. In verse 40 he told the king, "*And as thy servant was busy here and there, he was gone.*" Often that is what happens in human relationships. It is easy to get so busy doing the "things" we need to do that we forget about the people with whom we come in contact as we are "busy are here and there."

2. Live your life on purpose. Be aware of the people around you and give them the "hug"—whether an actual embrace or a kind word or deed.

3. Marlene Evans often stated, "People are more important than things." She influenced thousands of lives because she lived that principle. Make the people in your life more important than any "thing."

Mark and Sheri Edwards, graduates of Hyles-Anderson College, serve in Teays Valley Baptist Church in Hurricane, West Virginia.

He Fills Our Mouths With Laughter

by Leslie Beaman

As a home economics teacher, I have really tried to make an effort through the years to encourage my family to eat right. I have pushed vegetables, salads, fresh fruits, drinking water, etc. Sadly, I have to admit that I've "caved in" in a few areas. Yes, I confess my younger son really likes cereal, and I have become his willing supplier. Yes, I know there would probably be more nutrition if he ate the cardboard boxes the cereal came in. I guess I've hoped the vegetables I've pushed on him throughout the week would offset his time-to-time breakfast fix. Anyway, back to my story.

One day last week cereal was on sale big time. I mean the store I go to was practically giving it away! (Well, almost!) Anyway, I bought several different kinds and smuggled them into the house. When my younger son opened up the pantry door, he turned to me with a big smile, and I said, "The Cereal Santa made a visit."

My older son, not to be outdone, quickly quipped, "When is the Ice Cream Santa coming?"

I, of course, laughed and inevitably thought of Marlene Evans.

Mrs. Evans loved to laugh! Humor was probably one of her most endearing qualities. She was always so happy and upbeat. I have laughed longer and harder in one day with Mrs. Evans than most people do after watching a week of sitcoms on television. She had a way of making a bad situation not seem so bad. Rainy days were opportunities to jump in puddles or start a fire in a fireplace. Whenever she sensed someone was nervous at meeting her for the first time, she always smiled and said something to break the ice. Usually any awkwardness would quickly fade away.

I remember going on car trips with her in the summertime. It would be 90° outside, and she'd roll down all the windows, open up the moon roof, turn on the air conditioning full blast, and announce, "Now this is living in luxury!"

She also had a strange habit of making roads where there weren't any. Defiantly she would drive her car into places where even a 4x4 Hummer wouldn't venture! This was usually because she wanted to follow a deer into the woods. I remember driving around with her one day looking for tornado damage. I still don't know what exactly she was looking for, but it sure was fun!

Some of the funniest times were "getting lost"—something she did a lot. She'd be deep into a conversation and pass an exit and then laugh as we spent hours finding our way back.

I also loved to make Mrs. Evans laugh. Once she picked up a line from an *Anne of Green Gables* book that went something like this: "Precious little in this world amuses me, but Anne girl, you amuse me!" She used to say it to me from time to time when I did something she thought was funny. I would have to say after all these years, I still miss her. I miss her laughter. I miss laughing with her. Precious little in this world amuses me, but Marlene, old girl, you **amused** me!

I know we all live busy lives. I know many of us have heavy burdens from time to time, but I believe humor is one of the tools God has given to us to help lighten our hearts and keep our joy intact. If only we would use it more often....

1. One of the greatest evidences of a Spirit-filled life is joy. Galatians 5:22-23 says, *"But the fruit of the Spirit is love, joy,*

peace, longsuffering, gentleness, goodness, faith, Meekness, temperance: against such there is no law."

2. Laughter is a medicine. Proverbs 17:22 says, "A merry heart doeth good like a medicine: but a broken spirit drieth the bones." A merry heart is a medicine not only to a sick body, but also to a broken heart, emotional hurts, etc.

3. A sense of humor is a gift from God. Use it to show the world that being a Christian is the most exciting life one can choose.

This favorite snapshot of Marlene Evans shows her tremendous ability to have fun and enjoy life.

(Marlene Evans with Leslie Beaman)

Be a Different Woman!
by Frieda Cowling

Twice a semester Mrs. Evans took me to ladies' meetings to speak. I always believed that the ladies wanted to hear her, not me; I went along as "filler." This was fine with me. Her goal was to help me be a more effective speaker, but my goal was to enjoy the opportunity to spend time with her.

We went to Pastor Kirby Campbell's church in Marysville, Washington. My daughter, Krysten Vestal; her pastor's wife, Mrs. Vicki Mutchler; and a group of ladies from their church came to the meeting. I stood for my first talk, put on my glasses to read the Scripture, and noticed my daughter looking at me in an unusual way. (I didn't know if my slip was showing, if I had murdered the King's English, or if my hair was in disarray. But I knew that something upset Krysten.) I talked on, and when I had finished, I walked down to Mrs. Evans' chair. Krysten got there as fast as I did and exclaimed, "Mom, where did you get those glasses? They make you look like Grandma Moses!"

I was reared in the "use-what-you-have" school. I explained that I bought them at Wal-Mart's glasses rack. I stood the proper distance from the reading chart and tried on glasses until I found the correct strength for me. "What's wrong with them? They help me see."

Krysten replied, "You may be able to see with them, but they are the most unflattering glasses I could ever imagine."

I didn't say anything, but I was thinking, "These are perfectly good glasses. I paid $20 for them, and I don't plan to replace them until they are broken or lost."

I let the subject drop. I thought, "Krysten lives in Oregon and will forget about the glasses because she doesn't see me, and Mrs. Evans is too busy fighting cancer, teaching her classes, and traveling around the country to be concerned about my glasses." WRONG AGAIN!

The next Monday I received a call from Mrs. Evans. "Carol Tudor told me they have some stylish glasses at Walgreens. Why don't you go over and try them on? I'll call back tomorrow to see if you were able to get them."

I went to Walgreens and bought the glasses—not because I thought I needed them, but because Mrs. Evans was convinced that I needed them. It was easier to "switch than fight." Because she loved me and wanted the best for my life, I knew she would keep calling until I changed the glasses!

While some might think that switching glasses was solely a matter of vanity, it was exactly the opposite. Mrs. Evans understood what many Christian ladies do not. Dressing in a first-class manner will help increase our influence. She understood the teachings of Titus 2:3-5 which says, *"The aged woman likewise, that they be in behaviour as becometh holiness, not false accusers, not given to much wine, teachers of good things; That they may teach the young women to be sober, to love their husbands, to love their children, To be discreet, chaste, keepers at home, good, obedient to their own husbands, that the word of God be not blasphemed."*

Several important lessons can be learned from this experience. Three characteristics of a different woman are (1) a different woman is teachable, (2) a different woman will take correction from her godly leaders, and (3) a different woman realizes the importance of her appearance.

Deuteronomy 14:2 says, *"For thou art an holy people unto the* LORD *thy God, and the* LORD *hath chosen thee to be a peculiar people unto himself, above all the nations that are upon the earth."* That word *peculiar* does not mean "strange" or "weird"; rather, it means "valued property."

1. A person who refuses to accept correction will not grow or reach her potential. A key to being a growing Christian who influences others for eternity is being able to accept correction without defending yourself or trying to get others to sympathize with you by criticizing the leader for the correction she gave.

2. Mrs. Evans believed that a woman's appearance was important. She believed that we should look our best while staying within our budget. She believed it was important to be in style without being extreme or faddish. She felt looking our best was a part of being a different woman and would open more doors for us to influence others for eternity.

3. We are children of the King of kings. Our appearance should reflect our status as daughters of the King. Psalm 45:13-14b indicates that our dress ought to be different than the typical sloppiness or manliness so common among the unsaved, *"The king's daughter is all glorious within: her clothing is of wrought gold. She shall be brought unto the king in raiment of needlework."*

God Colors My Hair

by Frieda Cowling

I loved Marlene Evans, I know she loved me, and she knew that I loved her. God used Mrs. Evans to influence my life more than any other woman with the exception of my mother. Her dreams and goals for me by far exceeded those I had for myself. When I had no desire to accomplish her goals for me, she refused to take "No" for an answer! Most of the time I eventually gave in because of her persistence and her love for me. I can only remember one time I did not agree to please her, and that one area had to do with coloring my hair.

I had dishwater blond hair, and the gray became more and more prominent as I became older. This fact became a concern for Mrs. Evans. Her first plan of action was to have my two daughters speak to me about coloring my hair. I explained my feelings to my daughters. The following are two of my issues:

1. I really have nothing against hair color, but my observation was that some people looked very good with colored hair when they were willing to pay the price to keep it in good condition.

2. Others I noticed had one color at the roots and one color at the ends—not an attractive look. Because I don't like to spend a lot of money on maintaining my hair, I could see myself in this—not a pleasant prospect for me.

I further explained to my daughters that they were responsible for giving me my gray hair, and it was there to remind them of all I had gone through to rear them!

I thought that was the end of the issue! She continued to make suggestions. Her arguments were as follows:

1. "It will make you look younger." (She called my gray hair "old" hair!)
2. "You don't have to spend a lot of money. You can get a box from the store and do it yourself."
3. "You can change it back if you don't like it."

I countered these three suggestions with more of my personal observations:

1. "I believe God can do a better job of coloring my hair than I can, so I have decided to let Him color mine."
2. "Having attractively colored hair requires a greater commitment of time and money than I am willing to give."
3. "I have observed many 'do-it-yourself' hair color jobs that look worse than gray."

Her campaign to get me to color my hair was unsuccessful. We had reached an impasse, but it did not mean Mrs. Evans was giving up. In my case, she did not make a suggestion and forget it. She kept bringing up the hair color issue again and again. After two years of hearing her "hair-color campaign," I accompanied her to a ladies' meeting.

After one of the sessions where she listened to me speak, she said, "I have decided you were right in deciding not to color your hair." That announcement meant so much to me since I had always tried to follow her advice. To this date, I do not know what made her change her mind, but I am glad she did. I loved her and had a desire to please her.

However, there were many other issues that she refused to forget and "continued her campaign for change" until I was willing to follow her advice! I wanted to please her because I realized she loved me and desired God's will for my life. Today I owe her a debt I can never repay.

Never Underestimate the Value of One Black Skirt

by Kristal Slager

Loretta Walker called to ask if I could drive Mrs. Evans to a meeting at Pastor Cecil Ballard's church in Iowa. Of course I was overjoyed to spend time with her. We made arrangements to leave on Friday morning. Mrs. Evans spoke on Friday night, and we were then treated to a fantastic dinner. (I was treated like the royal court for the princess, and I was just the driver!)

After Mrs. Evans spoke at the first session on Saturday morning, I went to the guest room where she was resting to see if she needed anything. She was talking with her dad, Alvin Zugmier, who lived in Kearney, Nebraska. After getting off the phone, she explained that his health was failing fast, and he worried her. I asked, "How often do you get to see him?"

"Not enough." She hadn't seen him in two months.

With wanderlust in my bones, I quickly stated, "Let's go! We're halfway there now!"

She just looked at me and said, "Are you serious?"

"Of course I am!" She immediately picked up her phone and called her sister Doris to get her feelings on how serious their dad was and on her making the trip. I heard Mrs. Evans assure Doris that I was competent. (Ha! I did not burst her bubble with the truth!) Mrs. Evans then called her husband and ASKED if it was okay. (That was a great lesson from Mrs. Evans; I am sure that most people assumed since she was such a great lady that she did not have to seek her husband's approval. I am also sure Mrs.

Evans knew her husband would, of course, want her to see her father.) Her actions impressed upon me that no matter how busy or how in demand she became, she still sought her husband's approval on the matter of her being away longer than planned. Dr. Evans asked how she was feeling and then acquiesced to her request to go for the visit. After she completed her speaking engagement, we would take off for Kearney, Nebraska.

Her health was at a stage when she easily became tired physically. Mrs. Evans didn't want those helping her to have added burdens. Therefore, she planned her wardrobe in a way so that her help wouldn't have much to carry. Mrs. Evans wore a black skirt and blouse on the trip. She had a matching jacket to wear when she was to speak. She then had a dressy blouse to wear with the same black skirt on Saturday. All of this "wardrobe coordinating" was just another one of her ways of thinking of others. Although I was perfectly capable of carrying luggage, she didn't want to cause extra work for me.

On the other hand, knowing I was carrying my own luggage, I took plenty of clothes. I wore a cotton dress to drive in on Friday, changed into a dressier dress for Friday night, had a suit to wear on Saturday, and yet another simple cotton blouse and casual skirt to wear driving home on Saturday night. Of course, this was before the trip took a detour.

We left for Kearney and arrived late in the night. During the trip, Mrs. Evans called to find out about Sunday services. We were all set! We would check into a motel, sleep a few hours, go to church, and then she could spend the day with her dad. I told her I was going to shop. Really, I was going to shop for a shady park to sleep in! I did not want her to waste her time with her father by playing hostess to me.

Sunday morning we woke up. Mrs. Evans bathed; then I bathed, and when I came out of the bathroom, Mrs. Evans was lounging on the bed in her robe. "What are you doing?" (I thought we were pressured for time.) She started hemming and hawing—which was so unlike her! Finally, she asked, "What are you going to wear?" She wasn't the kind who was concerned about what others wore—if it was clean and modest, it was good. She did not judge others on their brand of clothes.

Knowing that, I wondered, "Why does she care what I wear?" I opened my suitcase and pulled out the nice blouse and casual skirt and said, "This." I wondered, "Is she concerned I will cast aspersions on her good name by being too casual for church?"

With a twinkle in her eye, she said, "I thought you looked really great in the dress you wore to drive up here on Friday."

I said, "Okay, I could wear that," again thinking that she thought my blouse and skirt were too casual.

She then added, "I was thinking maybe I could wear your last clean outfit; it would look really good on me!"

I started laughing; I had forgotten that we were now on day three with Mrs. Evans still wearing her black skirt!

You guessed it! She wore my blouse and skirt; I wore my cotton dress, and we looked great! By the way, we smelled good, too! We didn't worry about someone seeing us wearing the same clothes all weekend. When we arrived in Schererville, I helped her get into bed, and she said, "Take your clothes home with you; I might forget to give them back."

After Mrs. Evans' father went to Heaven, she sent me a note thanking me for taking her to see him. It was the last time she saw him alive. Oh, yes, I learned the value of a good black skirt!

Much can still be learned from someone like Marlene Evans who struggled with cancer for 19 years, all the while living the victorious, abundant Christian life:

1. Mrs. Evans was not too proud to ask for help. She would never have accomplished all that she was able to do for

eternity had she not accepted help from those around her. She didn't just accept it; she often asked for the help of others. She realized that when others helped her, they were investing in eternity. She often said, "God knows fractions." She believed every helper would have a portion of the rewards for anything that was accomplished for eternity in her life.

2. She was very careful in her treatment of those who helped her. She realized that it was a privilege to have the help of these good people. She treated them with dignity, kindness, and generosity. Though she did not "pay" people to help her, she shared what she had and all that came her way—in the form of gift certificates, jewelry, calendars, perfume, special lotions and soaps, and more.

3. She was never demanding to those who helped her; she was always careful to ask if they could do something rather than demand or order them to do a task.

4. She made it fun, exciting, and interesting to help her—making those who helped her feel like it was a great privilege to loan an outfit or drive her for hours so she could visit her dad!

In 1972 the path of Marlene Evans and Kristal Slager would cross when Kristal was a young student's wife. Mrs. Evans never forgot Kristal and asked her if she would be available to drive her to meetings if needed. She knew Kristal was the kind who would putter around by herself and didn't need to be entertained. Mrs. Evans liked Kristal's sense of adventure and willingness to just go for it and not think of all the reasons why they should be cautious.

A Catastrophic Road Trip

by Kristal Slager

In the summer following the Homegoing of Alvin Zugmier, Mrs. Evans' father, she called me and asked me to take her to Kearney, Nebraska, to throw a surprise birthday party for her stepmother. Mrs. Evans' father had remarried after his first wife went home to Heaven. Mrs. Evans loved her stepmother and the wonderful care she had given to her father.

We were to leave on a Friday afternoon, drive all night, and arrive in Kearney on Saturday morning. Mrs. Evans had already made the arrangements for the party prior to our leaving. All that was needed was to drive 665 miles and show up for the surprise party at 12:00 noon.

We left on time. It was getting past midnight, and Mrs. Evans was comfortably sleeping in the car when I noticed that the headlights were dimming and the compressor on the air conditioner seemed to be sluggish. Being from a rural upbringing, I immediately thought, "The alternator is going out." I shut off everything that would pull power and started looking for an exit. We were 115 miles from Lincoln, the "big city." I saw an exit coming up for Seward, Nebraska, and I also saw a sign for a Motel 6. By now it was 1:00 a.m.

I thought, "I will get Mrs. Evans a hotel room and work on getting the alternator replaced." I was pretty sure I could make that happen. Just unbolt the alternator, unplug the "pluggy" thing, get a new one, bolt it on, and plug it in! Sounds easy, doesn't it? As I was pulling off the exit for Seward, I realized, "This is **not** a big town." Fortunately, the Motel 6 was right at the exit. Things were going well. Mrs. Evans stirred and asked what was going on.

I explained to her about the car and that I was turning into the motel. About that time, the car gave up the ghost, and we coasted into the motel.

As I went inside to get a room, the clerk sleepily came out from the back and told me they didn't have a vacancy. Oh, great! I still remained positive. After all, I was traveling with "Miss Rejoice in the Lord Always," wasn't I? I noticed a great couch in the deserted motel lobby. I went back out to the car to talk to Mrs. Evans. I explained that I would take her into the motel to sleep on the couch, I would wait until the morning, walk to the parts store, buy an alternator, install it, and we would still arrive in Kearney in time for the party.

Mrs. Evans said, "I have a motor club card."

I called her motor club, and they said they would send a tow truck from Lincoln, 115 miles away. We switched to plan B. Mrs. Evans would rest on the couch, and I would wait in the car for the tow truck. Mrs. Evans then let me know she need to use the "facilities." I went back into the motel. You guessed it—there were no public restrooms. Being the trooper that she was, Mrs. Evans stated that that was fine. Wanting to take good care of her, I insisted we would find a spot. I won't go into the intimate details, but if you ever hear a story about two women in the wee hours of the morning rustling through a lespedeza field in Nebraska, I am pretty sure it was someone else and not us! Mission accomplished.

Mrs. Evans went into the motel to rest, and I returned to the car. I was comfortably dozing on and off. I looked up to see Mrs. Evans walking through the parking lot. My first thought was, "She's worried about me." I noticed she was clutching something in front of her in her hands. I jumped out of the car and asked her what was wrong. She looked at me and said, "I've got the key."

"What key?"

She proceeded to tell me that when she was lying on the couch, a man came in, assumed she was the clerk, and said, "I am checking out; don't get up. I will leave the key lying here on the desk."

She said, "It is room 202," and took off walking. I caught up with her and asked, "What are you talking about?"

She said, "I am going to room 202 and use the washroom."

I went back to the car to wait for the tow truck and Mrs. Evans. I waited, and I waited, and I waited. By then I was getting nervous. I started walking toward the back of the motel.

Keep in mind that it was about 2:30 a.m. and pitch-black. I came around a corner and ran right into her! We got the giggles, and it is a wonder we didn't wake up the entire motel. She asked, "Do you want to use the washroom?"

I decided it might be a good idea since I had no idea how long it would take before the tow truck arrived. We crept up the stairs to room 202. Once in the room, we noticed that it looked as though the gentleman had hardly used the room. The towels hadn't been touched, the bed was barely mussed. I said, "I'm going to take a quick shower."

"I'll lay on the unmussed side of the bed while I'm waiting for you," she said.

When I was finished, she was fast asleep. I knew she had to be exhausted, so I left her there and went back to wait in the car.

About 3:30 a.m. the tow truck came into the parking lot. I got out of the car and explained to the driver that I needed to go get my passenger in "her room." He proceeded to hook up the car while I got Mrs. Evans. We got into the tow truck to drive two hours back to Lincoln, Nebraska, to get the car fixed. It was a small cabbed truck, so I got in the middle to keep Mrs. Evans from having to climb across the seat. The situation was like something out of an old horror movie.

The gear shift was between my leg and his. I was crowding Mrs. Evans to keep my legs away from the gear shift. The truck gave a bouncy, rough ride. He was talking and asking questions about what we were doing out in the middle of the night with Indiana plates. I proceeded to tell him that Mrs. Evans worked for a Christian college and that she spoke all over the nation. You know, I wanted to emphasize that if he killed us, she would be missed! I explained that we were on our way to Kearney for a surprise birthday party.

He said to Mrs. Evans, "So you're a preacher, huh?"

I was geared up to witness to him and just said, "Yes, and let me ask you a very important question. If you were to die tonight, are you 100% sure you would go to Heaven?"

I didn't even realize that I had stated that Mrs. Evans was a preacher! Later we had a good laugh about that! He stated that he didn't know for sure he would go to Heaven. I figured we had two hours in a tow truck with a man in the middle of the night in Nebraska. So I proceeded to lead him to the Lord starting in Genesis and winding my way down to Revelation! That had to be the longest presentation of salvation I have ever given. I figured we would keep talking about Jesus in case he thought we were cute or rich! He was so sweetly saved. He said, "This was the luckiest tow call of my life."

We were heading east and backtracking 115 miles from our destination; the sunrise was so beautiful that Mrs. Evans became quite animated. The tow truck driver said he would deliver her car to a mechanic. He gave me phone numbers, directions, and everything I would need to pick up the car. He was so kind and gracious to us. He took control of our "helpless women" situation. He didn't take advantage of our beauty or money like I had feared. He said, "I'll take you to a restaurant in downtown Lincoln that is open early, and the car rental facility is one block down from the restaurant. It will open at 8:00 a.m."

I ran the numbers and figured, "If we get the rental car and get back on the road, we are only 133 miles from Kearney, and the party is at 12:00 noon—3 hours max. We are in great shape!"

When you traveled with Mrs. Evans, she wanted to enjoy EVERY aspect of the trip and not be encumbered with details—especially the detail of money. She always gave you her wallet of money and had you care for everything. Once we arrived at the restaurant, she became so excited. She exclaimed, "When I was a young girl, I always wanted to eat at this restaurant!"

We ate breakfast and waited for the car rental agency to open. When we arrived at the car rental agency, I made the arrangements and handed the gentleman her driver's license and credit card. He filled out the paperwork, looked at me, and said, "Of course, Marlene, you are the only one who can drive the car. You do understand that?"

I nodded my head and never mentioned that I wasn't Marlene. I didn't mind answering to her name. I surely wasn't going to make a sick lady drive!

Off we went, headed for Kearney with time to spare. Mrs. Evans made a point of teaching me a valuable lesson on that ride. She mentioned that she had recently been to a birthday party for Linda Stubblefield's daughter. She said, "It disturbs me when people talk to each other instead of the guest of honor. When celebrating someone's birthday, wedding, or whatever, the guest of honor should receive all the attention." Her point was that when we arrived in Kearney, we would never let on to her stepmother about all the problems we had encountered on our trip there. Wasn't that a wise thought? She wanted her stepmother to receive all the attention and never know about the kind of trip it had been.

We arrived, and the party was great! Mrs. Zugmier never knew what we had encountered getting there. We were almost tripped up though. Mrs. Evans introduced me to her stepmom as someone who took her places. After the party, Mrs. Zugmier wanted to go to the store.

As we were walking toward the car, Mrs. Zugmier saw the

rental car, noticed it had Illinois plates, and said, "I thought you were from Indiana."

I could honestly say, "I am, but my husband is originally from Illinois."

Mrs. Evans, wanting to get the most out of the trip, had made plans to meet family in Lincoln at the Cracker Barrel for a late dinner that same evening. The plan was I would drop her off at the restaurant, return the rental car, have them drop me off at the mechanic's, pick up the car, return to the restaurant, and pick her up to head home.

Keep in mind, we were now pushing 24 hours on the road, and I hadn't yet slept. I was getting a little slap-happy, to say the least. At the car rental agency when I returned the car, everything was in order. When I told the gentleman where I needed to be taken, he looked a little concerned and said, "You can't just be dropped off in that part of town; it isn't safe."

"I'll be fine," I assured him.

He was so gracious and said, "I will have someone stay with you to be certain the car is ready."

I must say it did appear to be a rather seedy side of town. I stepped into the garage, and I was assured that the car was ready. I waved for the driver to go on. As I was paying for the car repairs, a huge Rottweiler began to circle my legs—sniffing. I am not really thrilled with dogs to begin with, and this dog was huge! The person taking my money said, "Yeah, the tow truck driver brought in this car and said someone from this car told him how to go to Heaven. Was that you?"

I have to tell you, 24 hours with no sleep, a huge Rottweiler circling my legs, and Mrs. Evans waiting on me made me tempted to say, "What? Going to Heaven? That must have been someone else." Of course, I didn't. I pulled out my New Testament and told him he could know too. I proceeded to tell the same story that has been told for generations. He too accepted Christ and then said, "My buddy just went to the 7-11 to get us a sandwich. He will be right back. Can you wait and tell him this too?"

"Of course, I would be glad to!" Isn't that what I was supposed to say? I sat on the curb and waited. The huge Rottweiler soon brought his friend—an even larger Rottweiler—out of the garage to wait with me! Did I mention that I am not really a "dog person"? Soon the mechanic's friend returned, and he too accepted Jesus! Isn't it wonderful how God chooses the everyday problems in our life to show us His purposes?!

I was soon off to get Mrs. Evans. As I stated before, Mrs. Evans always wanted her traveling partner to handle the money and details. She was at Cracker Barrel (without any money), entertaining her family members. She had a niece with her. When I arrived, she was still visiting with her relatives, and her niece was getting restless. Mrs. Evans asked me to go out into the Cracker Barrel store and let her niece pick out a gift. The girl purchased a Beanie baby and a CD of "Elvis' Greatest Hits." Mrs. Evans saw us returning to the table and immediately became animated. In her effervescent way, she began giving all of her attention to her niece and asked excitedly, "What did you buy?"

The girl proudly pulled out her Beanie baby and the Elvis CD from the bag. Mrs. Evans acted ecstatic about her choices!

We left the restaurant after hugs goodbye from her family and headed for home. I told Mrs. Evans about the mechanic's being saved. She started rejoicing! I waited with trepidation for her to "talk" to me about spending her money on "Elvis' Greatest Hits." She ran down the family chain of how her guests related, she talked about her love of Cracker Barrel, she told me about her love of using paper bags as briefcases, she told me how glad she was she had surprised her stepmother...I still waited. "When is she going to, in her kind way, tell me that I shouldn't have spent her money on 'Elvis' Greatest Hits'?" I wondered.

You know what? We passed out of Lincoln into Omaha, from

Omaha into Iowa, and she still reveled in the great time she had and how wonderful God was to use our trip to see folks saved.

Finally, I opened the conversation by saying, "I probably shouldn't have spent your money on an Elvis CD," and boy, was I taken aback by her reply.

She explained that often she had been looked upon as thinking she was better than some of her family members because of her standards and convictions. She said the mending and the fellowship she had with her distant family members at Cracker Barrel, along with purchasing the niece a gift of her choice without condemnation, was just wonderful. She taught me that if she had objected to that CD, all she had accomplished with them would have been for naught. They would have only remembered that part of her being judgmental about their daughter choosing an Elvis CD. She used these words, "I will choose my battles based on how Jesus will benefit."

She added that she wouldn't have offended them for the world if it would cause them to look down on her testimony for Jesus, and that Elvis CD was trivial compared to souls. She did point out that she didn't think the CD was appropriate for her niece to listen to, but it was important that the door be open for her to listen to Jesus.

What a lady! Was it a horrible trip because of all the obstacles we encountered? I don't think so!

I learned so many lessons on our catastrophic road trip:
1. Make the guest of honor the most important person of all.
2. Never miss an opportunity to tell someone about Jesus... Rottweilers or not!
3. Don't be so offended by people's actions that you cause them not to hear the Holy Spirit over your objections.

My Memory of Marlene Evans
by Tina Lashbrook

"Wait up!" I wanted to call. I could hardly keep up. My seven-month pregnancy girth was slowing me down a little as I hustled to stay up with Marlene Evans. We finally made it to the gate, and with a smile and a hug, she boarded her plane. Whew! Mrs. Evans did not let things in life pull her down, slow her down, or cause her to lose her attitude of always rejoicing in the Lord.

As I went with Mrs. Evans to the airport that day, I asked questions and listened to her answers for an hour or so. She shared how she still went soul winning even when she could only walk short distances. She told me how she would go to the mall, find a place to sit, and her partner, Fay Dodson, would bring people to sit and "talk" with her. There really are no excuses for not being a soul winner.

We also talked about the professional basketball finals with Michael Jordan and Dennis Rodman. She was taken by the way the team worked together even when there were major differences in the team members. Mrs. Evans related what she had seen to church members and how we should all work together for the same goal—even with all our differences.

When we reached the airport, the airline representative had difficulty with processing Mrs. Evans' ticket. She and another helper waited at the counter for over an hour while I waited with the car. When the other helper rushed to the car, she said, "Make sure you see her get on the plane," and she took the driver's seat.

Then came the mad rush to the gate—her energy level could only be supernatural! What a sight to see an expectant mother trying to keep up with her. Hardly anything stopped Mrs. Evans!

Her zest for life and her determination to "live until she died" kept her going through the hard times and is still an encouragement to me through mine!

1. One day Marlene Evans was struggling to decide whether she should purchase a new pair of black orthopedic shoes. She knew she might not have long to live, and she hated to spend $150 on a pair of shoes she might only wear a few weeks. Though she lived for several more years, she made a statement that day that she put into practice until her death on July 8, 2001. "I'm just going to live until I die!" she declared.

2. We would all do well to "live until we die." Rather than staying focused on the cancer, the chemotherapy, the long trips to Mayo Clinic for treatment, etc., Marlene Evans decided to focus on what she could do. Through the hard times, focus on what you *can* do.

3. "Living until you die" does not mean to live in denial. Address the issues such as getting cancer treatment, but once you have done all you can do, put all of your energies on what you can do for eternity. Positive thoughts create energy. Energy begets energy. Negative talk and negative thoughts sap energy. They are energy robbers. Keep focused on the positive things you can do.

Both graduates of Hyles-Anderson College, Tina Lashbrook and her husband Pastor Tony Lashbrook serve at the Lighthouse Baptist Church in Ashland, Wisconsin. Tina served as a dormitory supervisor under Mrs. Evans.

Time-Released Teaching
by Frieda Cowling

On two occasions, my husband and I hosted a trip to Tennessee for Christian Womanhood winners and Mrs. Evans to "my Smoky Mountains" (as she called them). I have many wonderful memories of these trips, but one special time was an afternoon driving around Roaring Fork. This is a nature drive beside the river near downtown Gatlinburg. Mrs. Evans had told us to bring along a quilt, and we brought one without knowing exactly why we needed it.

As we drove this picturesque trail, Mrs. Evans said, "I'm looking for the perfect place to stop." She soon found it, and we disembarked from the van, got the quilt, and walked through the woods to a spot beside the river. It was nice there, but I was wondering what she was doing since we had a full schedule of events. (Sitting beside a stream on a quilt was not included in our itinerary, but Mrs. Evans had a different idea, and she knew best.)

At first, we just sat in the woods on the quilt, soaking in the beauty around us and listening to the music of nature and the river. After a few minutes, I stopped looking at my watch and "got with the program."

Soon we started asking the master teacher questions. She answered candidly and practically on how to deal with criticism, how to love the unlovable, and how to go on when your heart is breaking. I have forgotten many details of this trip, but her answers have helped me repeatedly just when I needed them. We sat at Mrs. Evans' feet as many sat at the feet of Jesus.

Marlene Evans is now in Heaven, but the truths she taught me come back to me when I need them.

When we teach others Bible truths or when we learn Bible truths ourselves, we may feel frustrated as it sometimes seems the teaching doesn't "take."

1. It is important to keep in mind that we have a big God who uses the truths we have learned when they are needed. His Holy Spirit can bring the Biblical truths we need to mind just when we need them. Isaiah 55:11 says, "*So shall my word be that goeth forth out of my mouth: it shall not return unto me void, but it shall accomplish that which I please, and it shall prosper in the thing whereto I sent it.*"

2. Though it is important to live by schedule and keep commitments, sometimes spontaneous happenings are times that can be used to really help others.

3. When a leader departs from the schedule at hand, "get with the program" and support the diversion. It may change your life!

Frieda Cowling first met Marlene Evans when she invited Mrs. Evans to speak at a mother-daughter banquet in Chilicothe, Illinois. At that meeting, Mrs. Evans taught "The Five Sins of Christian Women." Afterward, Frieda went to Mrs. Evans and asked if it was wrong for a woman to wear pants. Mrs. Evans told Frieda that obviously she could be a good Christian, serve God, and wear them, but if she was interested in being all she could be for the Lord and pleasing Him, she would stop wearing them. Frieda found that it cost a lot to follow her advice, but it was worth it.

Marlene Evans—
The Atmosphere Setter
by Frieda Cowling

Philippians 4:4 says, *"Rejoice in the Lord alway: and again I say, Rejoice."* Being reared in a Christian home, I was taught to avoid complaining, criticism, and negative thinking. However, I considered myself a no-nonsense type of person and was about as exciting to be around as "watching paint dry."

God sent Mrs. Evans into my life to teach me that life was not to be lived for myself, but to bring joy and happiness to others. (All work and no play makes us dull and boring to be around.) Matthew 5:14, 16 says, *"Ye are the light of the world. A city that is set on an hill cannot be hid. Let your light so shine before men, that they may see your good works, and glorify your Father which is in heaven."*

Everywhere Mrs. Evans went, she brought an atmosphere of excitement. Several years ago we lived in a house with a flood plain behind it. The raccoons would come out of the woods, tip over the garbage cans, and scatter garbage over the backyard. My husband quickly tired of this, so he would throw anything raccoons liked to eat in the backyard. They would come to the backyard every night when my husband threw out the food and called, "Here, raccoons." We enjoyed watching them with our grandchildren.

In passing, I mentioned our raccoons to Mrs. Evans, and you would have thought she had struck gold. "You can call raccoons; they come into your backyard and eat?!" She exclaimed, "I've got to see this for myself!"

Not long afterward, Mrs. Evans came over to see the raccoons. My husband moved our easy chair in front of the window and fixed a spotlight to shine on the raccoons. "This is wonderful," she exclaimed. "Let's count and see how many come. That big one must be the big boss. All the others make room for him...." And on and on. She changed the atmosphere to one of excitement. We forgot our troubles as we watched the raccoons. We also created a bond that knit our hearts because we belonged to the "Raccoon-Watching Society." We made such wonderful memories out of such simple happenings.

Thank you, Mrs. Evans, for enriching my life and showing me the importance of losing myself and creating an exciting atmosphere for others—even while watching raccoons!

A person who sets the proper atmosphere wherever she goes refreshes the spirit of those with whom she comes in contact. Several examples are given in the Bible:

1. I Corinthians 16:17-18 says, "*I am glad of the coming of Stephanas and Fortunatus and Achaicus: for that which was lacking on your part they have supplied. For they have refreshed my spirit and your's: therefore acknowledge ye them that are such.*"

2. In Philemon verse 7 Paul states to Philemon, "*For we have great joy and consolation in thy love, because the bowels of the saints are refreshed by thee, brother.*"

3. In II Corinthians 7:13 the Bible says, "*Therefore we were comforted in your comfort: yea, and exceedingly the more joyed we for the joy of Titus, because his spirit was refreshed by you all.*"

4. The previous three examples depict Christians who refreshed the spirit of others. It is important to keep in mind that nothing is stated about a person's personality.

The key issue is their spirit—their attitudes toward life.

5. A person's attitudes are a direct result of his thinking processes. A person who refreshes the spirit of others is a person who is controlled in his thinking. He does not allow negative, destructive thoughts such as jealousy, bitterness, anger, etc. to dwell in his mind. He fills his mind with Philippians 4:8 thoughts—*"Finally, brethren, whatsoever things are true, whatsoever things are honest, whatsoever things are just, whatsoever things are pure, whatsoever things are lovely, whatsoever things are of good report; if there be any virtue, and if there be any praise, think on these things."*

Marlene Evans Moments
by Nancy Musser

Not long ago someone who works in the printing world complimented some brochures my husband had printed. That simple act was so encouraging to us, and it reminded me of a "Marlene Evans moment" for sure. Her teaching on "time-released teaching" comes back to me time and again. Here are some of her teachings I am reminded of again and again.

- Find something good about someone and tell that person.
- If you hear something good about someone, pass it on to the person and/or to others.
- Give people what they want (attention, care, etc.—even if the person asks all the time)
- Find gold glittering (look for the positive in every situation) everywhere you go.
- Notice nature—cardinals, hummingbirds, blue herons, and deer.
- Let your husband shine. Quiet yourself when you are in public with him.
- Accept others for who they are.
- Have fun with the smallest things and make life a happening. (I tell young mothers this!)
- Take care of yourself.
- Love and study your Bible. Write in it.
- Let your married children be who they are. Don't try to change them. Let yours be the home in which they always feel comfortable.
- Have a cabinet of counselors around you to help you make wise decisions.

- Keep life simple.
- Laugh; it's good medicine.

Dan and Nancy Musser moved to the Hammond area to put their three children in the Hammond Baptist Schools system. Their entire family is involved in various ministries of First Baptist Church of Hammond. Nancy volunteered many hours to help Mrs. Evans in any avenue she could. Mrs. Evans felt free to call Nancy for help at any time because she knew Nancy was a faithful, "on-call" friend.

Honk...If You Love Coffee!
by Leslie Beaman

Yes, believe it or not, I saw a bumper sticker yesterday that said, "Honk if you love coffee."

You ask, "What did you do?"

"Well, I began honking my car horn!"

Now, I don't know if you can love something like coffee, but I sure do like it a lot! If my younger son had been with me, he probably would have dived for the car floor. He's never been fond of undue attention (unless he's causing it). Then a strange thing happened. The older woman driving the car with the bumper sticker got upset at me. How confusing! Didn't she know I was just enthusiastically agreeing with her?

I remember Dr. Jack Hyles' saying that most of the people who have a problem with people saying "Amen" in church don't seem to have a bit of a problem with screaming and cheering at a ball game. (Also confusing!) Maybe we as Christians have been made to feel so bad about showing excitement over the things of the Lord, we are afraid to react at all with any level of passion or enthusiasm.

When Steven Irwin, the great "Crocodile Hunter" from Australia passed away, the news played old interviews of him and his family members. On one such interview Steve Irwin was asked, "Steve, when you pass away, what do you most want to be remembered for?"

Without hesitation Steve Irwin said, "I want people to remember me as a passionate, enthusiastic conservationist."

Now I must admit that this interview caught my attention because this guy (Steve Irwin) was one of a kind!

If Marlene Evans were alive today, she would have called Steve Irwin a "maverick." That was her word for someone who was uniquely different. He was someone who stood out from the crowd in a colorful way. When the interview was over, I thought to myself, "If Steve Irwin could be that passionate and enthusiastic about conservation and wildlife, how much more should we as Christians be passionate and enthusiastic about the cause of Christ. I must admit I thought about those two words—passionate and enthusiastic—for days.

I believe Marlene Evans was a great teacher, leader, parent, wife, friend, writer, etc. because she put her all in everything she did. She was the most passionate and enthusiastic person I ever knew. She made everything she did seem like the most important or most exciting or the most fun thing anyone could ever do!

This is no excuse, but sometimes I think kids don't want to go into Christian work because they have spent too much time around Christian workers who have lost their passion and enthusiasm for their jobs. They have been around workers who gripe about what they get paid, the hours they have to work, etc.

I know people get tired. I know people get weary. But we need to always be aware that someone is watching. Someone is going to try to copy us. Will that be good?

Now, I don't believe I will be honking my car horn at any more "Honk if you love—" stickers, but I will continue to beg God to help me show others I am passionate and enthusiastic about the cause of Christ.

1. You are a role model to somebody—even if you don't think so!
2. Set an example so if someone copies your attitudes, actions, or appearance, it would please and glorify Christ.

3. Make sure you present the Christian life in a positive and happy way by the way you live. If you are happy to be a Christian (and you certainly ought to be!), let the world know it!

The Candy Jar Is Empty
by Leslie Beaman

A few years ago my mother passed away. I went to visit my father three weeks after my mother's funeral, and I brought my two sons with me. My younger son, as always, approaches life with a very logical, analytical view. He was very young at the time of his visit, but I'll never forget his first comments. When walking into my parents' living room, my son Adam said, "The music isn't playing, the candles aren't burning, the candy jar is empty—Grandma's dead." My mother was definitely the color in our home.

Marlene Evans was and always will be one of the most colorful people I've ever known. A visit to her house meant the sight of a burning fireplace, the smell of Yankee candles burning away, and the sounds of music playing. She really loved the sound of the piano and, of course, visits to the best restaurant in town. Mrs. Evans always wore "Beautiful" perfume, and to this day, I still turn to look for her whenever I smell that scent. Mrs. Evans was alive, exciting, and fun. She was "energy" even while dying with cancer.

In a black-and-white world, she was color. She was the brilliant pink and yellow and blue and purple and orange of life. She was a redbird, a sunset, a log cabin, a deer running through the woods, or a Bible well worn and marked up with a black Flair. She was a large bowl of popcorn with butter ready to be eaten while sitting by the fireplace on a rainy day. Mrs. Evans was sight, sound, taste, hearing, and touch. She lived a lot of life in one day, and she loved to teach about it. Mrs. Evans loved people, especially those who were needy. She was a giver and a servant.

So for me...the music isn't playing, the candles aren't burning, the candy jars are empty—Mrs. Evans is no longer alive. When I die, I pray with the Lord's help I will have made only one-half the impact on others that she made on me.

P. S. My dad now has a candy jar, and it's usually always filled.

1. Use the senses God gave you— taste, touch, smell, sound, and sight—to color your world.

2. Keep in mind your purpose for being here on this earth— to influence others for eternity. Use the five senses to make life more interesting and abundant for those around you.

3. In John 10:10b Jesus said, "...*I am come that they might have life, and that they might have it more abundantly.*"

Remembering Marlene Evans
by Joan Lindish

The following letter, which was written to Mrs. Evans on October 26, 1997, so captures the spirit and life of Marlene Evans that it begged to be included in this book. After all, the goal of this book was to capture the passionate life of Marlene Evans and to teach others how to make life happen—just as she did!

I have you on my mind so often—so just a note to tell you so. As I drive, I have been listening to your tapes. Some of them are from many years ago. Today I listened to you talk about "How to Communicate With Friends." I was greatly helped and will follow your counsel. The truth is, Mrs. Evans, though you may one day change your location, those who remain will always have you with them. You have given away so much of yourself in your books and tapes, you will never be more than an arm's length away. They can pick up your books and read your words or play your tapes and hear your voice. People will still be able to glean from your wisdom and share your laughter, which is contagious! I know it is— I've caught it!

Thanks so much. You are special, rare, uncommon! You are like a shell that has been tossed and turned in a mighty ocean, causing it to be unique and different from the other shells. Then one day a wave deposits it upon the shore where it is sought after because of its beauty and uniqueness. There are millions of shells on the shore, but only a few can be found that are rare and treasured by those who find them.

God made a living shell to house the spirit of Marlene Evans. The storms of life have often tossed and battered the shell, but what a lovely treasure to be desired and sought after has resulted.

Please keep fighting, keep living, keep teaching, and keep loving people. The ocean of tears may toss and change your shell, but your heart is unmoveable, fixed on Jesus. I will be forever grateful to you for your steadfastness, courage, and example.

I just wanted to bring you inside my heart and mind for a few minutes while I thought of you.

In 1972 when Dr. Jack Hyles founded Hyles-Anderson College, two of the first employees hired were Marlene Evans and Joan Lindish who, through laboring together, soon forged a lifetime friendship. Joan Lindish has taught secretarial courses at Hyles-Anderson College for many years.